THE CHURCH
UNDER THE CROSS

William Powell Tuck

THE CHURCH
UNDER THE CROSS

William Powell Tuck

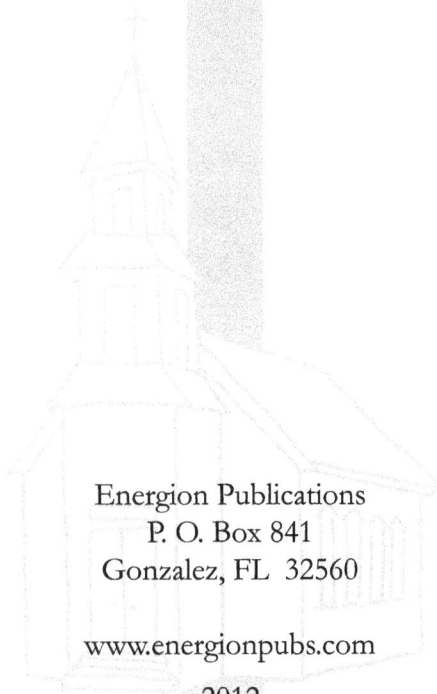

Energion Publications
P. O. Box 841
Gonzalez, FL 32560

www.energionpubs.com

2012

Cover Design: Nick May

ISBN10: 1-893729-21-4
ISBN13: 978-1893729-21-6
Library of Congress Control Number: 2012931957

TO

Paul and Betty Simmons

GOOD FRIENDS THROUGH THE YEARS

TABLE OF CONTENTS

FOREWORD

We live in a day when the cross is an offense to the religious sensibilities of many people, including many Christians. Churches have removed the cross from their buildings, because of its offense. Discomfort with sacrificial language connected with the cross has led to some to abandon the Eucharist. On the other hand there are those who simply see it as a piece of jewelry, and thus another golden idol.

The cross is a symbol that has defined the church since its earliest days, and despite the ambivalence of so many with it in today's church, it is the sign under which the church exists. This is true because the church exists as the body of the one who suffered and died upon a Roman cross.

William Powell Tuck brings his long experience as pastor and preacher to this conversation, reminding us through this brief but impressively thorough meditation what the cross means to the church and to the lives of those who inhabit the church. With his skillful guidance we are enabled to begin reengaging with the cross of Jesus, through which God reveals God's self to us and reconciles us to God's self. From this revelation and because of this reconciliation in and through the cross, our witness and presence in the world is empowered.

For those who seek a church with no strings attached this book will not offer good news, but for those who seek to find a church that is willing to follow God's leading and sink itself in breaking new pathways, and follow in the footsteps of Jesus wherever God chooses to lead us – without restrictions – this book will prove to be good news.

Bob Cornwall

PREFACE

Without question, the cross is the central symbol of Christianity. But the centrality of the cross is far more than symbolic; it represents a finality—an act of God. As Paul is bold to claim, "God was in Christ reconciling the world to himself" (II Cor. 5:19). Through the central act of the cross, Jesus died once for all for the sins of humanity. Paul and other New Testament writers put the cross at the heart of their preaching and teaching. Paul declared that he delivered to the churches what he had received from earlier Christians how Christ died for our sins (I Cor. 15:3 and 11:23).

Many today wonder what the death of a prophet from Nazareth, who lived two thousand years ago, has to do with them. "What could be its relevance for me now?" they ask. But I think F. W. Dillistone is correct when he boldly states in his book, *The Christian Understanding of Atonement*, "Indeed I am confident that there is no doctrine of the Christian faith which has more points of contact with life in the modern age."[1] The cross of Jesus addresses our emptiness, aloneness, suffering, pain, rejection, sins, alienation, and the questions arising out of God's silence.

The variety of images which Paul used to write about the death of Jesus shows that the cross touches life at many places. It is my prayer that those who read these pages about the cross of Jesus will sense anew the point of contact which this cross makes with their lives. The cross of Christ is not merely an ancient event which occurred two thousand years ago, but curiously affects our present situation today.

William Law captured the truth of the centrality of the cross over 200 years ago in the following words from *A Serious Call to A Devout and Holy Life:*

> The Christian's great conquest over the world is all contained in the mystery of Christ upon the Cross. It was there, and from thence, that He taught all Christians how they were to come out of, and conquer the world, and what they were to do in order to be His disciples. And all the doctrines, Sacraments, and institutions of the Gospel are only so many explications of the meaning, and applications of the benefit, of this great mystery.[2]

The major work on this book has been struggled with and revised over many years. Some special study was done while I was on a sabbatical from my church, St. Matthews Baptist Church, Louisville, Kentucky, where I was fortunate to be able to spend about a month in Oxford for study and travel. Through the graciousness of the former principal of Regent's Park College, Dr. Barrie White, I had opportunity to use the resources and quietness of the college's library. I am grateful to them for the privileges which they afforded me during that time. While at Regent's Park, I came across the book by the Principal of Regent's Park, Dr. Paul S. Fiddes, *Past Event and Present Salvation: The Christian Idea of Atonement.* I found his study most helpful. H. Wheeler Robinson stated that "the final test of a doctrine of the atonement is in its capacity to be preached; can it be turned into the necessary simple message of the evangelist?"[3] Here in these pages I have attempted to do that very thing. I have pointed to the cross of Christ and beckoned to fellow travelers along life's way to see the measure of God's love which has been revealed there.

I want to express my appreciation to Carolyn Stice, my former secretary at St. Matthews Baptist Church, Louisville, Kentucky, who helped translate my original renderings into readable print. I want to express special appreciation to Linda McNally for her careful proofreading of the manuscript. I also want to thank three of my former professors at Southeastern Baptist Theological Seminary at Wake Forest, North Carolina, Dr. James Tull, Dr. Stewart Newman, and Dr. John Eddins, all now deceased, for stretching my mind to grasp the mystery of the death of Jesus Christ.

THE CROSS
AND THE GOSPEL PARADOX

A number of years ago at an ecumenical conference, several ministers and priests who were involved in the program were sitting on the platform awaiting their turn. One of the priests, who had already spoken sat listening half-heartedly to another preacher who was speaking. He would glance up occasionally at the speaker. The priest wore a gold chain with a crucifix on it around his neck. An observer in the congregation noticed the priest absentmindedly cleaning his fingernails with the corner of the crucifix while he listened.

To me that action is symbolic of what has happened to our understanding of the cross. We have become casual and indifferent to its message. We really do not want much emphasis placed on the cross anymore. People want the church to focus primarily on celebration, peace of mind, comfort, and how to find freedom from worries or problems. Today we have chocolate crosses, candy crosses, and flower crosses. We try to disguise or avoid what the ancient cross meant and continues to mean today.

THE CROSS WAS AT THE CENTER OF THE PREACHING OF THE EARLY CHURCH

When one studies the Scriptures, there is no question that the cross was at the center of the preaching about Jesus Christ in the early church. A cross-shaped cavity was found in the wall of an upper room in Pompeii which was destroyed by Vesuvius in A.D. 79. About twenty inscriptions of the cross were found in the catacombs at Rome which scholars date in the second and third centuries. In most of our churches the cross is still the central symbol of the Christian faith. The cross is the symbol which is placed in the altar, in stained glass windows, and on the steeple of the church.

In some church traditions a cross is woven into the stoles or other vestments which are worn by the minister. In some worship settings the choir processes in and one of the ministers or someone else may carry a processional cross. Some church buildings are constructed in the shape of a cross. Crosses are sometimes imprinted on Bibles, hymnbooks, and other religious books. We sing about the cross in our hymns. The cross is depicted in poetry, art, sculpture and in many other ways.

THE CROSS IS THE CHURCH'S CENTRAL SYMBOL

Without question, the cross is the church's central symbol. Yet many people are very uncomfortable with what the cross symbol really means. It has become an offense once again to many.

Jürgen Moltmann, a renowned German theologian, wrote the following lines in his scholarly book, *The Crucified God*:

> The cross is not and cannot be loved. Yet only the crucified Christ can bring the freedom which changes the world because it is no longer afraid of death. In his time the crucified Christ was regarded as a scandal and foolishness. Today, too, it is considered old-fashioned to put him in the centre of Christian faith and theology. Yet only when men are reminded of him, however untimely this may be, can they be set free from the power of facts of the present time, and from the laws and compulsions of history, and be offered a future which will never grow dark again. Today the church and theology must turn to the crucified Christ in order to show the world the free-

dom he offers. This is essential if they wish to become what they assert they are: The church of Christ, and Christian theology.[4]

The renowned theologian is reminding the church once again that the cross must be at the center of our faith. Although I have preached many times on the cross, I always stand before it with trembling voice. I struggle to put into words the mystery and awe which encompass this event. John Milton, who wrote "On the Morning of Christ's Nativity" in celebration of the birth of Jesus, tried to write a similar poem about the cross but finally gave up. There is a mystery about the cross which we can never get a handle on completely. Anyone who says he/she fully understands what has happened at the cross and can explain it sufficiently to somebody else really does not understand the New Testament mystery of it.

THE CROSS IS PARADOXICAL

The cross represents a paradox. A paradox is a statement that is seemingly absurd or contradictory. The cross seems inconsistent with common experience. It is paradoxical because it depicts man/woman at his/her worst and best. It denotes foolishness and wisdom, a victim and victor, an historical and eternal dimension. A mysterious paradox surrounds the cross and the gospel message which is proclaimed about this cross. As we attempt to understand the New Testament message on the cross, let us begin by examining Paul's paradoxical statement that the cross is both foolishness and wisdom (I Cor. 1:18-24). Paul noted that the cross to the Jewish mind was a scandal. No Jew expected the Messiah to end up on a cross. The Jewish law stated: "Cursed is he that hangs on a tree" (Deut. 21:23). It was a curse to be crucified. The crucifixion was clear evidence to the Jews that Jesus was not the Messiah. They were looking for a political Messiah, someone who would come in with military might and strength of arms to overthrow the Roman rulers.

THE SCANDAL OF THE CROSS

All of this talk about Christ crucified as the Messiah was to them a stumbling block. The words in Greek for "stumbling block" literally mean a trap or snare. To the Jewish mind, the thought of a crucified Messiah was a trap that was simply unacceptable. Paul persecuted the early Christians himself because he could not accept this teaching.

In one of Dostoevsky's novels, the Russian author has a scene where a man is seen standing before a painting of the crucifixion. "Don't look at that picture, you fool," another character cries, "Don't you know a man can lose his faith by looking at that picture?" "Yes," the man replied, "That is just what is happening to me."

The cross was seen as such a scandal that the Jewish people rejected any notion of a crucified Messiah. To the Greeks, the concept of a crucified God was considered just plain foolishness. The Greeks prided themselves in their rational knowledge and logical understanding of life. The word "foolishness" is derived from a Greek word which is the root for our word moron. The Greeks ridiculed anyone who believed that a crucified carpenter could bring salvation.

The disdain which the Greeks held for the cross was depicted in a painting that was discovered on an ancient wall. When the plaster was removed, a figure was seen hanging on a cross. The figure had the body of a man and the head of an ass. Underneath were written the words, "Alex the Jew worships his god." This kind of disdain and ridicule was directed at the early Christians by the Greeks because they believed that the concept of a crucified Christ was totally absurd.

THE CROSS AS THE POWER AND WISDOM OF GOD

But Paul is bold to declare that what seems a scandal and foolishness to others, when understood properly, is the power and wisdom of God. The cross is the power of God because it is an expression of God's sacrificial love. Although it sounded foolish, Paul affirmed: "Unto us which are saved it is the power of God." Paul preached that God's strength was made perfect in Paul's weakness. The cross event revealed God's power in a unique way. God's power is consistent with God's character. God does not exercise raw power, or try to coerce or force people to love him, but he draws people to him by love.

In the Upper Room Jesus gave his disciples a strange picture of power. He, knowing that all power in heaven and on earth was his, took a towel and a basin and washed his disciples' feet like a slave (John 13:3-11). His power was dedicated to service. Jesus said on another occasion, "Whoever would be chief among you, let him be the slave or servant of all" (Matt. 20:27). In Jesus, God's power was focused in the form of a servant. This is disciplined power—the power of sacrificial love.

The New Testament is filled with many images which the various writers employ to depict the power of God which was revealed in the cross of Christ. Paul used the image of justification which he took from the law courts. He drew pictures of redemption and emancipation from the slave market, reconciliation from the image of friendship, adoption from family life, propitiation or ransom from the sacrificial system of Judaism, sanctification from their worship practices, and the view of setting a person's account right from the accounting system. Many theologians have built their theological system around one of these pictures.

A VARIETY OF IMAGES INTERPRET THE CROSS

But the New Testament does not give just one interpretation of Christ's death on the cross. There are many. A casual glimpse into the New Testament discloses images of Christ's death as sacrifice, substitution, metaphors drawn from the law courts, expiation, forensic, satisfaction, example, revelation, deliverer, representative, suffering servant, lamb, and many others.

No single one of these images contains all of the truth about what God has done in Christ's death. All of these images underscore the great mystery involved in the God who has loved and redeemed us on the cross. The cross can never be reduced to images of legal, judicial, transferring of guilt, paying off a debt, contracts with the devil, appeasing an angry God, etc. All of these images are just illustrations of the power and mystery of what God has done in Christ on the cross. No one of these pictures can contain the whole of the mystery.

THE CROSS AS THE WISDOM OF GOD

The cross is not only the "power of God," according to Paul; it is the "wisdom of God" as well. Unlike many itinerant Greek teachers of wisdom, who emphasized rhetoric and eloquence, Paul declared that he proclaimed "an unadorned gospel." The Greeks wanted something that would satisfy the mind, but the images of God on a cross blew their mind. The wisdom of God which Paul is describing could never be reduced to some system of beliefs about God or to a set of propositions. But it was the wisdom which was personally revealed through Christ's death within history.

The word "mystery" was not a reference to something that remains unknown or a puzzle, but refers to that which was previously unknown. The reference is to the redemptive work of God in Christ. Something which was previously unknown about God's nature has been revealed through the death of Christ. "To those who have been called, both Jew and Greek, Christ is the power of God and the wisdom of God, for the foolishness of God is wiser than men, and the weakness of God is stronger than men." In a unique way Christ has revealed the power and wisdom of God's love.

THE CROSS AND SIN

The cross also reveals to us something about the ugliness of sin. Sin is so costly that God's Son went to the cross to lay down his life for us. We are all too familiar with our own sense of sin. We are never free from it.

You may have seen the *Peanuts* cartoon where Lucy walks over to Snoopy one day and says, "Hold my balloon. I'm going to lunch." She sticks the string in his mouth and walks away. He sits there holding onto the string with his teeth, and the balloon is floating above his head. A few minutes later he falls asleep. When he awakens suddenly, he yawns and lets go of the string. The balloon drifts off as the wind carries it up into the sky. In the last scene Snoopy is walking down some railroad tracks with a little parcel on his shoulder. "Make one mistake," he observes, "and you have to regret it all your life."

Many of us go through life with a sense of regret over mistakes which we have made, and wonder what we can do to overcome these feelings or find forgiveness. The good news of the gospel is that you and I never have to try to overcome our sins with our own strength. Through God's grace, revealed in the mystery of the cross, we find forgiveness and the opportunity to begin anew.

A small boy went to church for the first time on Sunday. He saw a cross on the altar and nudged his mother and asked: "Mother, what is that plus mark doing on that table?" That may not be a bad image to use to describe the cross. The cross is God's "plus" mark which reveals his affirmation, love, grace, and forgiveness. Yes, the cross is a paradox. It is foolishness to those who think that they can solve all of life's problems with their own efforts and strength. But it is also the mysterious wisdom of God's love and atonement.

JESUS AS VICTIM AND VICTOR

The cross is a paradox because it reveals that in his death Jesus was both victim and victor. The New Testament states that Jesus' life was both taken and given. The cross represents suffering and triumph, defeat and victory, horror and glory, wickedness and sacrifice. The cross shows that in one way Jesus was a victim. He was betrayed by Judas. He was rejected by the religious leaders, scourged and put to death by Roman officials. The cross depicts murder, betrayal, and rejection. "The stone which the builders rejected," Jesus said, "has become the head of the corner" (Mark 12:10). The New Testament clearly states that Jesus was betrayed and murdered. (See Acts 2:23; 2:36; 7:52; 13:28; I Thess. 2:15-16).

From one perspective the death of Jesus was a life that was taken, but the New Testament never leaves it there. The biblical writers are bold to declare that he was not just a victim but a victor. They believed that he was in charge of what was happening. Listen to the words of Jesus himself: "For this reason the Father loves me, because I lay down my life that I may take it again. No one takes it from me, but I lay it down of my own accord. I have power to lay it down and I have power to take it again; this charge I received from my Father" (John 10:17-18). Then in Mark's gospel Jesus said, "The son of man also came not to be served but to serve, and to give his life a ransom for many" (Mark 10:45).

On another occasion Jesus said: "I am the good shepherd and I lay down my life for the sheep" (John 10:15). When he was approaching Jerusalem, Jesus looked down on the town and wept saying: "O Jerusalem, Jerusalem, killing the prophets and stoning those who have been sent to you! How often would I have gathered your children together as a hen gathers her brood under her wings, and you would not" (Matt. 23:37). Jesus wept over Jerusalem, but there is no indication that Jerusalem wept for him.

After Peter's confession at Caesarea Philippi (Mark 8:29), Jesus warned his disciples that he had to suffer and die. Following the transfiguration, at the Last Supper, and on other numerous occasions, Jesus told his disciples that he would go to Jerusalem and die. But they never seemed to hear or understand his prediction. It was only after the resurrection that his disciples began to sense what he had taught them. When Jesus, the risen Lord was walking with two of his disciples on the road to Emmaus, he said: "Oh fools, and slow of heart to believe all that the prophets have spoken. Was it not necessary that Christ should suffer these things?" (Luke 24:25-26). Then he opened the Scriptures to them and interpreted from the prophets and other writings the prophesies of how the Messiah must suffer many things. Have you ever wondered what particular passages Jesus must have shared with those disciples that day? Did he quote from the Psalms, Jeremiah, and Isaiah?

Paul, writing later to the Corinthians, declared: "For I delivered to you as of first importance what I also received, that Christ died for our sins in accordance with the Scriptures" (I Cor.15:13). Jesus was not merely a victim; he was also a victor. The Old Testament Scriptures do indeed predict the suffering One—who would be God's Messiah. Yet Israel did not seem to look for such a Messiah, but what other image could one draw from Isaiah? Isaiah's image is clearly about a Suffering Messiah. Listen to the verbs alone in Isaiah's passage about the Suffering Servant in the fifty-third chapter. He will be marred, recoiled, shut-mouthed, avoided, afflicted, bore our sufferings, endured our torments, smitten by God, struck down by disease and misery, wounded, bruised, chastised, crushed, oppressed, dumb, stricken to death, numbered with transgressors, bore the sins of many, offered for sin, poured out his soul, and made his grave with the wicked. The verbs disclose something about the suffering, sacrificial nature of the One who would give his life. These verbs vibrate with the heartbeat of a Suffering One and are not the vision of a militant king.

SACRIFICE AS A VITAL PART OF THE CHURCH'S LIFE

Suffering has always been at the heart of the life of the Church, and that is still true today. Sometimes we want to put sacrifice on the back burner, but we really cannot and be the Church. I am convinced that nothing really worthwhile ever comes about in life without some kind of sacrifice. To serve or reach worthy goals there has to be some sacrifice of time, energy, effort, or money, and sometimes even one's life.

Recently when I was visiting a church member, who had been ill, his wife told me about a couple in our church who had visited them recently. She spoke kindly of this visit and of how much it had meant to them and observed how many others they visited. I thought about the numerous lives this couple touched because they were willing to sacrifice some time to visit the sick or shut-in. But they were willing to pay that price. The Christian gospel continues to focus on the necessity of sacrifice.

THE CROSS AS HISTORICAL AND ETERNAL

The gospel writer also denotes that there was both an historical and eternal dimension to the cross. In one way, the cross is an historical event, because there was a certain date, place, and time where Christ was crucified. The date was approximately A.D. 30. Jesus was crucified on the garbage dump outside Jerusalem at Golgotha. Outside the city gate, Jesus was crucified between two thieves. George McLeod of Iona reminds us of the historical nature of the cross in these words:

> I simply argue that the cross be raised again at the center of the market place, as well as on the steeple of the church. I am recovering the claim that Jesus was not crucified on a cathedral between two candles, but on a cross between two thieves; on the town's garbage heap, at the crossroads so cosmopolitan that they had to write his title in Hebrew and in Latin and in Greek, at the kind of place where cynics talk smut and thieves cursed and soldiers gambled . . . That is where he died and that is what he died about.[5]

Christ died in a particular place at a particular time. But the Scriptures are also clear that Christ's death was not merely an historical event, but there was an eternal dimension to the death of Christ. God did not suddenly become loving at the cross in the death of Jesus. God has always been a loving God. The book of

Revelation states that he was "the Lamb that was slain from the foundation of the world" (Rev. 13:8). Here is the image of the cross which was always at the heart of God before it was planted on a hillside. The cross discloses the heart of God. The cross provides a clear picture of a God who is eternally loving and caring. Jesus did not have to persuade God to love men and women and be reconciled to them, but he revealed instead that his death was to persuade us to be reconciled to God who already loved us. God's work of redemption continues into every age.

This is the truth Emil Brunner noted when he wrote:

> The Atonement is not history. The Atonement, the expiation of human guilt, the covering of sin through His sacrifice is not anything which can be conceived from the point of view of history. This event does not belong to the historical plane. It is super-history; it lies in the dimension which no historian knows in so far as he is a mere historian.[6]

As we reflect on the cross, it tells us about the death of Jesus in a particular place, at a particular time, but the cross also reveals to us a God who is continuously loving, redeeming, and suffering and who makes his grace available to us today.

Paul said the Jews seek a sign—a miracle and the Greeks want wisdom, but . . . We preach Christ crucified. We—everyone—who proclaims the message of salvation—testify, bear witness to Christ. We witness to a person, not a philosophy or a system of theological thought. We preach Christ crucified. He is not just an example, or teacher, or martyr. We preach Christ crucified—God's Suffering Servant who laid down his life for us.

Following the death of Victor Hugo, the noted French author, there was a riot, and the French people secularized the Pantheon. They pulled the gilded cross down, because they wanted to remove all evidence of Christianity from the building. A Christian orator stood up and tried to stop them from pulling the cross down. "You think you can take away the cross from the Pantheon," he cried. "We have taken it away," they shouted. "We've torn it down."

"You'll never take away the cross from the Pantheon," the Christian orator shouted. "It is taken away, and down with the church," they yelled. After the shouting died down, he stated quietly: "You cannot take away the cross from the Pantheon, for the Pantheon is built in the form of a cross, and when you have taken away the cross, there will be no Pantheon anymore."[7]

To remove the cross from Christianity is to destroy the Christian message. The cross is at the center of our message about Christ. If we remove the cross from Christianity, we do not have the genuine New Testament message. With the hymn writer Isaac Watts, we proclaim:

> When I survey the wondrous cross
> On which the prince of glory died,
> My richest gain I count but loss,
> And pour contempt on all my pride.
> Forbid it, Lord, that I should boast,
> Save in the death of Christ, my God.[8]

2

THE CROSS AND THE FACE OF GOD

One of the unique features about the Christian religion is that
its founder died a violent, sacrificial death at a very young age. This
kind of death was not true of other great religious leaders. Moses
died when he was an old man as he looked over into the Promised
Land from Mt. Nebo. Buddha died at the age of eighty. Confucius
was in his seventies, and Mohammed was in his sixties when he
died. Zoroaster was seventy-seven and died a violent death at the
hands of the Turanian invading army which killed him and many
others when they plundered the city. The Christian faith is unique
among the world's religion because it puts the death of the Son of
God, who willingly laid down his life, at the center of its belief. On
one occasion, Jesus declared: "No one takes my life from me, but
I lay it down of my own accord" (John 10:18). "I have come to
serve not to be served and give my life as a ransom for many"
(Mark 10:45).

One of the most powerful passages in the New Testament on
the Incarnation and death of Jesus Christ is found in Paul's Philippian letter, chapter two, verses 5-11. Without hesitation I would
state that this passage is one of Paul's deepest theological insights.
Some of his most profound thinking is reflected here, along with
lofty eloquence. But this passage has also been a storm center of
theological debate. As scholars have struggled with this difficult
passage, controversy has surrounded almost every line.

In a few pages I hesitate to approach the deep theological message set forth here. I feel like someone who has scaled a high

mountain and arrived at the top breathless, with his head dizzy from the effort, and now trying to get his bearings. This passage is a magnificent insight into who Christ was. It is different from the rest of this epistle. Its difference is so apparent that most scholars feel that it is really a hymn. Some scholars say that it has two strophes while others see three strophes in the tradition of the psalms. Scholars have debated whether Paul was quoting a hymn which was a part of the early church's tradition or whether Paul composed this hymn himself. Nobody knows for certain. Paul was certainly capable of expressing this kind of creative genius. He had exhibited this gift in other places like I Corinthians 13. There is nothing to demonstrate that this could not be Paul's own profound theological insights.

THE DIVINE NATURE OF CHRIST

As we begin to examine the magnificent message found in this hymn, note that Paul, first of all, focuses on the divine nature of Christ. "Who being in the form of God," Paul stated, "thought it not robbery to be equal with God" (2:6). The Greek language is a much richer language than English. The Greek language has several words to express a similar idea, while English usually has only one word. There are at least two words for "form" in Greek. One of these Greek words for "form" means appearance or shape. The other word means "what it really is in its essence." When I was born, I had a certain "personality" which was uniquely my own. This inner essence constituted who I really am. As I grew, I changed from a baby to a young boy, from a teenager to a man, and have continued to change outwardly each year. But the essence of who I really am as a person remains the same. The word "form" which Paul uses here about Jesus focuses on his inner essence.

In some special way, Christ shared in the essential quality of God's divinity. In his essence he was in the "form of God." I am not sure exactly what that means or how it is possible. There are several other places in Paul's epistles, in other New Testament writings, and especially in the prologue to the Gospel of John where there are references to the pre-existence of Christ (Col. 1:15; II Cor. 8:9; Heb. 1:1-4). "In the beginning was the word and the word was with God, and the word was God" (John 1:1). John A. T. Robinson, the English theologian, wrote a book several years ago on Christology and he entitled it *The Human Face of God.*

Lenore Johnson quotes an eleven-year-old girl in his collection of children's sayings. "Jesus is the part of God you can see," Elaine said.[9] Her childlike insight is something of the truth which Paul is wrestling with in this hymn. Jesus Christ has revealed to us something about the nature of God.

There is a painting which depicts Christ hanging on the cross. At first glimpse when you look at the painting, Christ appears to be alone. As you examine the painting more carefully, you are able to see another figure looming behind the figure of Jesus on the cross. The nails which go through the hands of Jesus reach into the hands of that other figure, too. The spear that is thrust into the side of Jesus is also thrust into the side of the figure behind him. The artist was trying to tell us that "God was in Christ reconciling the world unto himself." He was seeking to portray that on that cross there was not just a man hanging there, but in some way, God was in Christ. Rather than snatching or clutching at his relationship to his Father, Christ willingly laid it down for our redemption.

THE HUMANITY OF CHRIST

But notice secondly that Paul spoke about the humanity of Christ. He said Christ emptied himself. The Greek word for "emptied" pictures pouring something out of a container. Of what did Christ empty himself? He obviously did not divest himself of his divinity. Instead, as Frank Stagg notes, "He poured out his life to God in humble, obedient, self-denial—refusing in any way to act selfishly."[10] But he obviously emptied himself of omnipotence and omnipresence. Whatever else it may mean to speak of his divine nature, Christ was localized in a particular place and time. He was limited. He got hungry, thirsty, and tired. He suffered, bled, and died. He was a real human being and was not just disguised like one. Christ voluntarily emptied himself of some of his glory and became a servant.

Scholars have wrestled with the self-emptying (kenosis) of Christ, but the mystery has remained. I don't know how to explain the Incarnation, and it is not clear to me exactly what Paul is saying in this passage. But one thing is certain: Paul is focusing on the sacrificial nature of what God has done for us by identifying with us in human form.

Writers like C. S Lewis, Leslie Weatherhead and others, whom I can no longer recall, have used various analogies to try to give insight into the mystery of the Incarnation. One of these describes a man standing over an ant hill whose shadow falls across the ant hill and causes them to flee. The man's shadow intimidated them each time he drew near the hill. "I wish there were some way," he said to himself, "that I could communicate to them that I am a friend and I do not wish to harm them. Maybe if I became an ant, I could convince them." Suddenly the thought about the Incarnation came to him. Now, granted this is a crude analogy, and we need to remember that all analogies are weak and do not walk on all fours. But even its crudeness may help us to remember the great sacrifice involved in the Incarnation. The mystery may forever elude us. This emptying of himself denotes self-abasement and the supreme identification with human suffering.

Christ's self-emptying is revealed in his taking the form of a servant. Paul may have had in mind here the vision from Isaiah 53 where the Suffering Servant takes upon himself our stripes and iniquities, and through his sacrifice we are healed. Christ became a bond slave. He was obedient unto death, even the death on the cross. To be crucified on a cross was regarded as a great disgrace. No Roman citizen could be crucified on a cross and suffer that kind of indignity. It was against the law. Criminals, slaves, and outcasts—the rejects of society—were put to death on the cross. To die on a cross was the worst kind of disgrace a person could receive in ancient biblical times.

D. M. Baillie, in his monumental book *God Was in Christ*, reacts to the response of Jesus, "No one is good except God." Baillie contends:

> If we take the reply seriously, we shall surely find in it the supreme instance of that peculiar kind of humility which Christianity brought into the world. It was not self-depreciation: It was rather a complete absence of the kind of self-consciousness which makes a man think of his own degree of merit and a dominating sense of dependence on God. The Man in whom God was incarnate would claim nothing for Himself as a Man, but ascribed all glory to God.[11]

Christ called people to come to him so he could point them to God. He was obedient, even unto death on a cross.

Several years ago in Milwaukee a young man named Manuel Garcia had to undergo chemotherapy treatments for cancer. Like others who have had this treatment, his hair began to fall out in patches. His head was then shaved, and then he became very concerned about his appearance. His brother, Julio, recognizing his brother's concern, shaved his own head. Julio enlisted fifty relatives, friends, and neighbors to do the same thing. Later when visitors went to Manuel's hospital room, it looked like a bald-headed man's convention. This was one way Manuel's relatives and friends had to identify with him in his suffering and feelings of isolation.

JESUS IDENTIFIED WITH US

God in Jesus Christ came to identify with us. He became a man and lived out his life with the limits of human frailty. Paul didn't say Christ pretended to be a man. Rather he emptied himself of divine glory and took on human flesh. As John wrote, "The Word became flesh and dwelt among us" (John 1:14).

THE EXALTED SERVANT

Paul states further that Christ became the Exalted Servant. Paradoxically, Paul reminds us that the last has become first. The one who was servant has become Lord. The hymn changes here and God acts to exalt Christ. It is God who raised him up and Christ now sits at the right hand of the Father. What Jesus taught others about service, he incarnated in his life. He had proclaimed that "the greatest of all is the servant of all" (Matt. 23:11). He also declared that "he did not come to be served but to serve" (Mark 10:45). In another place Paul expressed this truth in these words, "For you know how generous our Lord Jesus Christ has been; he was rich, yet for your sake he became poor, so that through his poverty you might become rich" (II Cor. 8:9 NEB).

Paul also indicated that Christ would have a name which is above every name. Often in the Old Testament account of men's encounters with God, a man's name was sometimes changed because of that meeting. For example, Abram's name was changed to Abraham. Jacob's name was changed to Israel. Jesus himself said that he would give us (Christians) a new name (Rev. 2:17).

Christ's new name was Lord. In ancient time lord was a common title which might refer to a master, owner, political leader, emperor, ruler, or to the Hebrew word for Jehovah. This meant that Jesus Christ is Master, Owner, Ruler, Lord of lords, and King of kings. When a soldier took an oath in the name of Caesar, he pledged his loyalty to Caesar. He became Caesar's man. Likewise, a person who was baptized in the name of Jesus Christ indicated by that act that he pledged his oath to Christ and promised to follow him as master. The name of Christ carried with it the authority of his divine presence.

"Every knee," Paul said, "shall bow before him in heaven and earth, and under the earth. And every tongue shall confess that Jesus Christ is Lord, to the glory of God the Father" (2:10-11). The doxology affirms the earliest Christian confessional—Jesus is Lord. Jesus, the obedient servant, drew persons to himself that he might lead them to God. His sacrifice was to "glorify the Father."

Years ago I visited Copenhagen and had the privilege of seeing some of the sculptures of the famous artist, Thorwaldsen. One of his most noted statues is a figure of Christ who is standing with his head bent down so you cannot see into his face. When he first finished this statue, Christ was erect but the heat from the sun affected the newly shaped wax figure and caused the head of Christ to lean forward. The only way a person can look directly into the face of the Christ is on bended knees before the statue. But isn't that the way we should always come before Christ? We must bow before the One we acknowledge as Lord of Lords.

ADDRESSING DIVISIONS IN THE CHURCH

To me, the most remarkable feature about this particular passage is the reason Paul wrote it in the first place. When Paul quoted or composed this hymn, he was not concerned with some abstract theological treatise about God. This hymn was written to be directed toward a particular problem in the Philippian church. Their problem was disunity. The church was in turmoil because for some reason or another the church was divided.

In his commentary on Philippians Fred Craddock has observed that the division may have resulted from the polarization of two women who had worked faithfully with Paul in the church (4:2-3).[12] The division may have arisen from the Jewish element in the congregation who wanted the converts to become Jews first. They likely wanted to require that all males be circumcised before they could be officially members of the church. The controversy, however, may have centered on Paul. We don't know. Sometimes Paul was himself at the center of the controversy in his churches.

In the first part of the second chapter Paul urged the members of the Philippian church to unify and stop their divisiveness. He challenged them to end their discord. He charged them to put aside all selfish ambition, the seeking of personal prominence, and all attempts for self-gratification. Their desire for pompous, self-serving, conceited ends divided the church. His answer to this divisiveness was the example of the humility and sacrifice of Christ. This passage seems so lofty a goal to us that some might complain that Paul's effort was like shooting a missile to kill a squirrel. But Paul believed that the Philippian people would stop their quarrelling and self-seeking when they looked at the example of how God's Son humbled himself and became a servant, even unto death.

Paul was convinced that no Christian could be selfishly concerned about his or her rights, ways, interests, goals, or ambitions. As Christians, we, like our Lord, have been called to be servants. Our primary concern should not be what I can get out of religion, but what can I give in ministry. Christianity is not a summons to sit around and admire the cross of Christ. The cross is a way of life—the path of sacrificial living.

Paul lifted the example of the incarnate and crucified Christ before the Philippian church and he still calls us to follow the shining example of Christ. We are challenged to have the mind we saw in Christ who loved us to the point of sacrificial death. When we measure ourselves by Christ, we know we cannot be content with where we are spiritually.

It is easy for us to say: "Well, I am o.k. in many areas of life." You might think, "I am a fairly good artist." But compared to the artistic works of Michelangelo your efforts may look sketchy indeed. "Well, I'm not a bad writer," you might say. Then you compare your writing to Shakespeare and realize how inadequate it is. Or you might say: "Well, I compose fairly good music." But compare your compositions to Bach or Beethoven and you know how inferior they are.

It is easy to reach low goals. What is your spiritual standard? The One who emptied himself, became incarnate, and died on the cross, is our standard for love. His standard summons us to sacrificial love. His example calls us also to serve. "The greatest of all," Jesus said, "is the servant of all. I came not to be served but to serve." In Paul's letter to the Philippian church he set the example of Christ in front of them as the most powerful reason for ending their division. "Let Christ's mind be in you," Paul says.

When Frederick Buechner was a college chaplain he went to see the Italian movie, *La Dolce Vita,* in a college theatre one night. As the story began, a helicopter was transporting a life-size statue of a man dressed in a robe with his arms outstretched. The pilot occasionally flew down low over a field where some men were working on tractors. "Hey, it's Jesus," they yelled. Slowly the helicopter moved to the outskirts of Rome on its way to deliver the statue to the Vatican. The helicopter swooped down over some young women who were lying by a swimming pool and then hovered over them while the pilots tried to talk with them. The young people in the theatre continued to laugh and enjoy the frivolity of the moment until the camera began to zoom in on the face of Christ. The camera got closer and closer to the head of the statue until suddenly the face of Jesus Christ filled the whole screen. When that happened, Buechner observed that the theatre became deathly silent for a moment.[13]

The face of Christ needs to fill our lives and our minds. When it does, we have a completely different perspective on life. In some places in the Scriptures, face means presence. For example, the biblical benediction, "The Lord make his 'face' to shine upon you," is such a reference. Tennyson expressed this hope in his line, "I hope to see my pilot face to face"—to be in his presence. Let this mind be in you which was in Christ—the One who sacrificed all for us. Let us remember his sacrifice and live out our lives in sacrificial service.

3

THE CROSS AND THE SILENCE OF GOD

I wish I could tell you that all of your life will be filled with happiness and joy; you will never experience pain, have difficulties, disappointments, frustrations, or heartaches. That is a message we often hear from some. Some try to market this myth over the television, through the newspapers, magazines and books. These persons proclaim that life is principally positive thinking, possibility thinking, or being happy. This perspective says that we are primarily here to be entertained, to be excited about life, have fun, and go through life smiling.

But if I told you that, most of you would know that it is simply not true. You know that life is not always bright and beautiful. Sometimes it is dark and difficult. After all, you have known pain and suffering yourself. Many of you have experienced grief, and have witnessed the death of others. You have known rejection and misunderstanding. Some of you have stood by sick beds, hospital beds, and open graves. Some of you know the reality of cancer and heart attacks. We have seen or experienced famine, poverty, disease, or homelessness. We have seen the effects of tornados, hurricanes, earthquakes, volcanoes, floods and blizzards. What do we say about endless wars, terrorism, AIDS, and the horrors of Dachau, Auschwitz, and Mai Lai, of the massacre of students in Beijing, China or the massacres in Bosnia?

QUESTIONS ARISE

In the midst of the wintertime moments of life, many questions rise. Realistically we know that life is not all pleasure and happiness. There is a dark, stormy, north side to existence.

A Japanese writer named Shusaku Endo wrote a novel entitled *Silence* which describes the experiences of Japanese Christians during the early sixteen hundreds. One of the leading characters in this novel is reflecting on the persecution of the Christians and he observes:

> I do not believe that God has given us this trial to no purpose. I know that the day will come when we will clearly understand why this persecution with all of its suffering has been bestowed upon us—for everything that Our Lord does is for our good. And yet, even as I write these words, I feel the oppressive weight in my heart of those last stammering words of Kichijiro on the morning of his departure: "Why has Deus Sama imposed this suffering upon us?" And then the resentment in those eyes that he turned upon me. "Father," he had said, "what evil have we done?"
>
> I suppose I should simply cast from my mind these meaningless words of the coward, yet why does his plaintive voice pierce my breast with all of the pain of a sharp needle? Why has Our Lord imposed this torture and this persecution on poor Japanese peasants? No, Kichijiro was trying to express something different, something even more sickening. The silence of God.[14]

THE CRY OF JESUS FROM THE CROSS

Many voices are raised today asking: "Why is God so silent in the face of so much suffering and pain?" One place where God seemed the most silent was at the cross where Jesus Christ died. Jesus himself cried, "Eloi, Eloi, lama sabachthani." "My God, My

God, Why have you forsaken me?" The words, "My God, why?" have echoed down through the centuries. "God, why?" Why was God so silent at Jesus' cross? Only Mark and Matthew recorded these words from the cross. Luke recorded three other words and John recorded three different words which were not contained in the other two gospels. "Why have you forsaken me?" What provoked this outcry?

A Delirium Cry

Was it a cry of *delirium?* Did the physical pain and agony which Jesus suffered make him cry? Physical pain could certainly have made him ask: "God, where are you?" The 1986 spring edition of *The Journal of the American Medical Association* contained an article written by several doctors and ministers on the physical death of Jesus.[15] This article focused on the horror, agony, and suffering which he had to endure. There is no denying that his suffering was awful, but Jesus died relatively quickly on the cross. He died after hanging on the cross for only six hours. Some persons who were crucified in biblical times hung on their cross for days before they died. Other people have died more horrible deaths than Jesus. Yes, he suffered physically, but I believe that his cry contained more than the agony of suffering.

A Cry of Doubting

Was it a cry of *doubting?* Hanging on the cross, did Jesus ask himself: "Have I misunderstood my call?" "Have I been wrong about the mission of the Messiah?" Did this cry raise large question marks about the purpose for his life? Being crucified like a common criminal forced Jesus to rethink his mission. Were the mocking tongues right? Had he wasted his life?

A CRY OF DEPRESSION

Was it a cry of *depression*? Here, nailed to the cross, Jesus was isolated and rejected by his friends. Some members of his own family called him insane. Broken and misunderstood, maybe his spirits sank into deep depression. He saw his dream to bring in the Kingdom of God aborted. Was it a cry of *desertion*? All had forsaken him. Where was Peter at the cross? Where was Matthew? And Zacchaeus? Where was the centurion whom he had helped? Where was the once blind Bartimaeus? Where were the crowds of people that had pressed around him? Where were they now? Here he was deserted, isolated, alone.

A CRY OF DERELICTION

Was it a cry of dereliction? Was he abandoned by God at the cross as some theologians have suggested? Was it a cry of absolute isolation? Did God turn away from Jesus? A derelict ship is one that is abandoned by men and even rats. Did Jesus raise his cry against an empty sky? Was he in the depths of despair? Did the cross thrust him into the "dark night of his soul?" Was that the cause behind his cry?

Elizabeth Barrett Browning caught something of the agony in these words:

> Yea, once Immanuel's orphaned cry
> his universe hath shaken—
> It went up single, echoless,
> 'My God, I am forsaken!'
> It went up from the Holy's lips
> amid his lost creation,
> That of the lost,
> no son should use
> those words of desolation![16]

A Cry of Identification

But could the cry of Jesus have been one primarily of identification? That's what Carlyle Marney has suggested in his book *He Became Like Us.* "What if this cry 'My God, My God'" he suggests, "is not addressed to God at all?" He clarifies this further:

> What if he is not talking to God but to us? What if the "My God, My God, why hast thou forsaken me" is addressed to us "sitting down watching him there?" What if this cry is an appeal to us, not a cry to God at all? What if it is not a delirium? What if it is not a desolation? What if it is most certainly not dereliction? What if it is an identification?[17]

Here at the cross God was uniquely in Christ. At the cross we see God identifying with man/woman in their suffering. God was no place more present than at the cross. At the cross Jesus completely identified himself with our humanity as he suffered the consequences of humanity's sin.

A Misunderstanding of the Cry

Those around the cross misunderstood his cry and thought he was calling for Elijah. Muttered through painful lips, "Eloi" might be mistaken for the prophet's name. But insight into his cry might be found in realizing that the words, "My God, My God, why hast thou forsaken me," are likely a quotation from Psalm 22. These words begin the psalm, but Jesus may have quoted the whole psalm. Notice the last few verses of that psalm: "Praise him, you who fear the Lord, all you sons of Jacob, do him honor, stand in awe of him, all sons of Israel. For he has not scorned the downtrodden, nor shrunk from his plight, nor hidden his face from him, but give heed to him when he cried out. . . Let all the ends of the earth remember and turn again to the Lord. . . This shall be told of the Lord to future generations; and they shall justify him, declaring to a people yet unborn that this was his doing" (Ps. 22:23-24, 27, 31).

The final words on the cross were not "I am forsaken," a cry of despair, but a great shout of victory, "It is finished!" Forsaken was not the last word. There was a cry of identification which ended in a triumphant assurance of the presence of God.

OUR EXPERIENCES OF THE SILENCE OF GOD

But you and I have also known the silence of God, haven't we? There have been times in our lives when we, like our Lord, have had "why" well up within us. Sometimes why is a natural response to the sufferings of life. I have stood by the side of persons who were deeply committed Christians and heard the word "why?" form on their lips in times of distress, tragedy, illness, and grief. "What did we do to deserve this?" they ask. "Why has God permitted this to happen?" Or, "Where is God?"

Several years ago I conducted the funeral services for my brother's son, who was killed at the age of twenty-three in a motorcycle accident. As I stood in that funeral home chapel, I could hear echoing in my mind the questions of family and friends: "Why God, why? He was so young." Answers do not come easily.

Nicholas Wolterstorff has written one of the most moving books I have read in a long time entitled, *Lament for ｜Son*. His son was killed in a skiing accident in Austria when he was only twenty-five years old. In his struggle to understand his son's death, Wolterstorff, a Christian philosopher and professor, confessed:

> I have no explanation. I can do nothing else than endure in the face of this deepest and most painful of mysteries. I believe in God the Father Almighty, maker of heaven and earth, and the resurrection of Jesus Christ. I also believe that my son's life was cut off in its prime. I cannot fit these pieces together. I am at a loss. I have read the theodicies produced to justify the ways of God to man. I find them unconvincing. To the most agonized question I have ever asked I do not know the answer. I do not know why God would watch him fall. I do not

know why God would watch me wounded. I cannot
even guess. . . . I am not angry but baffled and hurt. My
wound is an unanswered question. The wounds of all
humanity are an unanswered question.[18]

There are times when the "whys" are painfully real. They are
your questions and they are my questions. For some, the sense of
the absence of God in the midst of such pain becomes almost
overwhelming. Martin Marty's wife died with cancer. Struggling
with his wife's painful illness and death forced Marty to an inner
quest for true meaning in such a crisis. spiritual journey is traced
in his book, *The Cry of Absence: Reflections for the Winter of the Heart*.
Digging into the Psalms for consolation, he discovered that over
half of the Psalms were reflections on the problems, difficulties,
and pains of life. He followed their "spiritual terrain of winter" in
search of an elusive Presence which took him on a slow journey
toward hope, sober faith and finally affirmation.[19]

THE SILENCE OF GOD CAUSES SOME TO REJECT GOD

There are some who are so convinced of the absence of God
in their pain, suffering or grief that they reject God altogether. In
one of Hugh Walpole's novels, one of the characters, who is a
young man asserts: "You know there can't be a God, Vanessa. In
your heart you must know it. You are a wise woman. You read and
think. Well, then, ask yourself. How can there be a God and life be
as it is? If there is one He ought to be ashamed of Himself, that's
all can say." The silence of God is so overwhelming for some in
their pain, suffering, grief, and death that they simply turn away
from God.

GROWING THROUGH SUFFERING

But there are others who look upon the world and realize that
you and I cannot be full and complete persons without the possibility of suffering. Can we really understand what health is if there

is no possibility of sickness? Can we really be courageous without the possibility of being a coward? Can there be saintliness without the possibility of being sinful? Can there be victory without the possibility of defeat? Can there be hopefulness without the possibility of hopelessness? Can there be faith without the possibility of doubt? I am convinced that without the possibility of suffering and pain, growth and maturity are not possible. Life is surrounded by this awesome mystery.

Wallace Hamilton records an experience he had on a vacation in the mountains one summer when his son was only four years old. His wife and the grandmother of the young four-year-old had gone off for a walk. He was supposed to be watching his son, but he was busy working on sermons and reading. The four-year-old, of course, became bored very quickly while his father was absorbed in his books. The four-year-old decided to go for a walk in the woods to see if he could find his mother and grandmother. Dr. Hamilton got up and followed his son at a distance. He knew he would get lost and he could have stopped him, but he didn't. The young boy walked almost a mile into the woods. From time to time he would look around and try to get his bearings, but finally frightened and exhausted he began to cry. Then Dr. Hamilton stepped out of the woods and walked up to him and asked: "Well, John, are we going home?" His son looked up, not in the least surprised to see him there, and said, "John's lost." And indeed he was.

Many times Dr. Hamilton said he reminded his son of that experience where he had given his son the freedom to go wandering off in the woods on his own. He had remained back in the shadows watching him make his way. It became for him a picture of the way God works in the lives of his children. "He (God) has made us persons, with all of the risk of it; persons free to choose the good and therefore also free to choose what is not good. He will not thrust Himself upon us. He will not impose His will upon our will."[20]

We could never really be fully human without the possibility of freedom. God has given us freedom to choose. But, as we live in the world, we have to obey the natural and moral laws of God's universe. Wherever there is free choice, there is always the possibility of pain or suffering as well as the possibility of good health. The possibility of suffering is as much a part of our universe as the reality of happiness and pleasure. This is the kind of universe we live in, and there are no easy answers to the mystery of our existence.

At the cross of Christ you and I discover that God gives us the same kind of answer in silence that God gave Jesus at Golgotha. Have you ever thought about how much silence surrounded the life of Jesus? When he was born, only a small number of people, a few shepherds and several Wise Men, knew of his birth. In one of our Christmas hymns we sing about this mystery: "How silently, how silently the gift is given." The Scriptures focus on only one episode in his childhood—when he was twelve years old in the temple at Jerusalem. What happened during that other period of his childhood? How silent the biblical writers were. Until the time he began his ministry at thirty years of age, there is nothing but silence about his young manhood. Most of his life is unknown to us. The Scriptures are silent.

Do you remember the story about the Syrophoenician woman who came to Jesus and asked him to heal her child, and Jesus did not answer a word? He was silent. When he stood before the high priest, Herod, and Pilate, he was silent. When he prayed in the Garden of Gethsemane, "My God, let this cup pass from me," he received only silence from God. When he hung on the cross and cried out, "My God, my God, why have you forsaken me?" there again was only silence.

GOD PROVIDES NOT ANSWERS BUT A PRESENCE

What does all this silence teach us? Maybe it reveals that God does not give us an explanation to the mystery of suffering and pain. Rather than an explanation, God gives us a presence. The answer is found in our awareness that God is in both good and evil.

The Book of Job struggles with the dilemma of suffering. Job discovered that there was no easy answer to the enigma of suffering. He was unwilling to ascribe all suffering as the result of punishment of sin. The biblical writers affirm that God is not only in the beautiful dimensions of life but is in the ugly and difficult as well. They affirmed God's presence in the flood as well as in a flower. God was present in the storm as well as in the sunshine, in plenty but also present in famine, in defeat as well as victory. All of life is under the sovereignty of God. Nothing separates us from his presence.

L. D. Johnson's daughter was killed in an automobile accident on an icy highway right after her twenty-third birthday. As he struggled to understand her death, he penned these words: "The mystery of unmerited suffering remains. I know of no satisfactory explanation. But for the Christian there is an answer——not an explanation . . . ." He pointed to the Incarnation, death and resurrection of Jesus Christ as the place where God's work of justification took place. Continuing, he noted that God:

> has not abolished the hurts of human existence, but he
> has shared them and identified himself with our plight.
> He did not change the order of the universe to make evil
> impossible and thus destroy man's humanity by taking
> away his freedom Instead he partook of the cup of
> suffering himself and gave us the promise that nothing
> in all creation can separate us from his love.[21]

God does not give us an answer to all of our questions. God gives us God's presence. God gives God's self to us in the midst of our struggles. Sometimes God's presence is discovered not in the noise around us but in silence. At the cross, God's great redemption is accomplished in that silent act of suffering. In the midst of our own pains, struggles, and difficulties we discover that we are not left to bear them alone but God is present. An ancient Christian writer Ignatius once wrote, "God affects more by his silence than others do with all their talking."

As you and I reflect on the cross, let us remember that God does not give us an explanation to the problem of evil, suffering, and pain but a presence. God has not forsaken us; God is always present. "Faith is a footbridge that you don't know will hold you up over the chasm until you are forced to walk onto it," Wolterstorff wrote.[22] When you walk on that bridge of faith, you will discover that in the most silent moments of your life's deepest pain, you are not alone, but the God who was in Christ on the cross is present also with you.

4

THE CROSS AND THE ATONEMENT

The death of Jesus Christ on the cross was a devastating blow to the early disciples. At first they simply could not understand why it had happened. The crucifixion of Jesus was such a scandal to them that they did not know how to deal with it. It was a stumbling block. They could not believe that the Messiah of God would be crucified. Yet, one-fourth of the material in the gospels is concerned with the death of Jesus Christ. His death soon became central in their preaching. The Apostle Paul, writing to the Galatians, declared: "God forbid that I should glory, save in the cross of our Lord Jesus Christ" (Gal. 6:14). The cross was raised as the central symbol of the faith.

Many years ago a monk told his church people that he was going to preach a sermon in the cathedral about the love of God and asked them to gather for the occasion of worship. At sunset the people slowly filed into the church to hear him deliver his sermon. The monk waited until the sun had set completely, and darkness slowly began to envelop the cathedral. The candles flickered in the darkness, providing the only light. After the people sat in silence for a long time, the monk went over and took one of the candles from the candelabra stand and walked over to the figure of the Christ hanging on the cross. He lifted up the candle flame and held it by one of Christ's pierced hands. Then he moved the candle to shine its light on the other pierced hand. Next he lifted the candle light by the pierced feet and then to the pierced side of Christ. Finally he cast the light on the brow where the thorns had pierced Jesus' forehead and then he sat down. The monk never said a word; yet in a powerful and eloquent way, he had preached a sermon about the love of God.

THE CROSS REVEALS THE NATURE OF SIN

The cross has drawn the eyes and hearts of men and women down through the centuries. Its mystery continues to demand our attention. The cross of Jesus reveals to us the nature of sin. The cross has disclosed that there was both love and hatred, sacrifice and sacrilege, a victim and victor in that awful event. God and humankind were both doing something at Calvary.

After the sinking of the Titanic, many newspapers carried drawings and editorial comments about the sinking of the world's largest ship and the loss of fifteen hundred lives. One newspaper had an editorial drawing of the Titanic sinking after it hit the iceberg. The caption beneath the picture read, "The Weakness of Man, The Supremacy of Nature." Right by that picture was another one of W. T. Stead, who sacrificed his life when he stepped back and let a mother and her child go into the last lifeboat in his place. The caption underneath read: "The Weakness of Nature, The Supremacy of Man."

The cross points both to the weakness of humanity—our sinfulness—and to the supremacy of God's love. The cross points vividly to our own weakness. Oh, I know that most people today do not want us to talk about sinfulness. "We are not going back and deal with that old foolish notion that men and women are sinners, are we?" some ask. We like to think that we are beyond that point today. We want to point to other causes as the reason for the foolish mistakes we make. We had rather point to weaknesses of character, heredity, environment, mental or physical disorders, etc. But we cannot dismiss so easily Mai Lai, Dachau, the massacre at Beijing, terrorism, war, murder, rape, child abuse, and "man's inhumanity to man" for these reasons. The only word that appropriately acknowledges the awfulness of many acts is sin.

THE CORPORATE NATURE OF SIN

The cross proclaims loudly and clearly the corporate nature of human sinfulness. The social sins of humanity nailed Jesus to that cross. The people who were involved in the events leading up to the death of Jesus reveals something about the nature of corporate sin. Judas depicts betrayal and treachery. Caiaphas symbolizes religious bigotry. The Pharisees stand for self-righteousness. Herod and Pilate denote graft, corrupt political power and injustice. The soldiers represent raw, military power. The crowd demonstrates indifference, apathy, and violence. The disciples reveal fear, rejection, and panic. These persons reveal the vivid nature of corporate evil. Oh yes, sin is real! It was sin that put Jesus Christ on the cross.

OUR OWN BASIC SIN

But sin is not limited to corporate sins. Sin is a reality of which every person needs to be aware and confess. Unfortunately, sin is a paramount feature of our nature. It is a foundational problem of human nature. There is a fragmented dimension within us. Sin has separated us from God, others, and from our authentic self. Our basic sin is pride, self-assertion, and self-love. Our central sin is what Reinhold Niebuhr called "God-almightiness." This is our desire to usurp God's reign in our lives. The deepest root cause of sin is self-centeredness. Sin, in the biblical sense, is missing the mark, or failing to fulfill what you have been created to be by God. Sin is failing to find the real source of life. Sin is the awareness of one's fragmentation within and without.

In South America there is a plant that looks like a bundle of dried up weeds. The plant is moved from one place to another by the wind. Whenever the wind rolls across a spot of moist ground, the plant will sink its roots down into that soil until it has used up the moisture in that piece of ground. After using up all the moisture in that soil, it is rolled along by the wind until it finds another moist spot. From there, it rolls along to another place. But it never looks like anything but a ball of dead weeds. Too often many live out their lives like that weed. They live selfishly off of others as they journey through life. They contribute little but demand much, give sparingly but expect to receive; take but seldom give.

MOST MAJOR RELIGIONS ACKNOWLEDGE THE REALITY OF SIN

Most of the religions of the world depict an awareness of sinfulness in their places of worship. When a worshipper enters the Jewish temple, he immediately acknowledges the holiness of God and confesses his sinfulness. The Hindu temple is constructed as though there were stages through which a person must pass in his quest of God. Successive courts suggest the search that occurs through body, soul, and spirit to escape one's sinfulness. The Muslims' mosque is designed like a man at prayer. The dome represents the head of a man, while the minarets depict his hands which are raised in prayer for the forgiveness of his sin. The Buddhist dagoba represents a man, who is unmoved, with his arms and legs crossed as he seeks to withdraw from the world to escape its sinfulness. All of the world's great religions acknowledge the reality of sin.

A cartoon appeared several years ago which depicted a salesman talking to a woman who wanted to buy a toy for her child. "This is an educational toy," he said, "to prepare the child for the modern world. No matter how you put it together, it's wrong."

There are many who live in the world with that kind of frustration. No matter what they do, it seems to turn out wrong. But the Apostle Paul, writing to the Roman church, declared: "There is therefore now no condemnation to those who are in Christ Jesus." (See Rom. 8:1-3). With a sound like a trumpet, Paul exclaims a celebrative note about the forgiveness of God through Jesus Christ. Paul's use of the word "flesh," denotes the sinfulness of humanity and its rebellion against God. Twenty times in the eighth chapter of Romans Paul refers to the "spirit" which suggests the mighty power of God's liberating and victorious grace.

In John Bunyan's *Pilgrim's Progress*, Christian climbs up the hill of Golgotha and stands before the cross of Jesus with the burden of sin on his back. As he stands before the cross, the burden-pack of sin suddenly breaks free and rolls down the mountain. He is set free from the load of his sin by the power of the cross. Paul's good news for his readers is the declaration that the cross of Jesus Christ has done something that we could not do ourselves. Christ has set us free. The cross of Jesus Christ has opened the door for us into the forgiving grace and presence of God. By faith you and I can cross the threshold into the presence of the forgiving, loving arms of God. The cross reminds us of the awful nature of sin.

THE NATURE OF GOD'S LOVE

But the cross also discloses something to us about the nature of God's love. The New Testament is filled with many images in an attempt to describe what God has done for us in Christ. Paul drew his images from the law court, the slave market, the accounting system, family life, and other places. But the writer of the Book of Hebrews, whoever he or she was, set his own picture. Note especially Hebrews 7:23-28. Some scholars believe that the writer could have been a woman. There are almost no scholars who attribute this particular epistle to Paul.

Whoever the writer was drew on the image of the Jewish sacrificial system to depict what God has done for humanity in the death of Jesus Christ. He pointed vividly to the Day of the Atonement which was the one day in the Jewish calendar when the high priest himself offered the sacrifice for the people. On that day the high priest went into the temple and first cleansed himself physically and then put on a spotless white linen gown. Then he offered a sacrifice for his own sin which he confessed to God. Having offered a sacrifice for his own sins, then he offered a sacrificial lamb for the sins of his people.

CHRIST AS SACRIFICE AND HIGH PRIEST

Drawing on this Levitical image, the writer of the Book of Hebrews depicted Jesus Christ as our great High Priest. But not only is he the High Priest, he himself is the sacrifice. Jesus represents the sacrificial Lamb of God. One of the vivid images in the stained glass window behind the pulpit in my church is the cross of Christ with a lamb in front of it, which was slain for our sins. Jesus drew upon Isaiah's vision of the Messiah as the Suffering Servant, the Lamb who was led to the slaughter. When John the Baptist saw Jesus coming for baptism, he pointed to him and said: "Behold! The Lamb of God who takes away the sin of the world." The one who forgave sin had to bear sin.

Jesus Christ, in John's Gospel, represented the Passover Lamb, the Paschal Lamb. This image is drawn from the Old Testament story about the Passover lamb which was slaughtered and the blood was put on the doorpost outside their house and the angel of death passed over the houses of the Jewish people. Jesus Christ was, in the image of John's Gospel, the Passover Lamb. Through his sacrificial death, we find forgiveness and grace.

There is another picture of the Lamb in the Scriptures. In the Book of Revelation the word lamb is used twenty-nine times. But this Lamb was not a victim but a victor. He is a conquering Lamb. The Lamb which was slain has now become sovereign reigning in victory and triumph.

Jesus is also the one "who can save to the uttermost." No matter what our sin is, this High Priest can bring us redemption. He said that he "came to call sinners to repentance."

In 1821 a Portuguese slave ship was filled with black men and women who had been enslaved in Africa. One young black man was brought before the slave market to be auctioned off. But he, like many others on that slave ship, was very sick. When the slave traders realized that they could not get any money for him, they tried to barter him for a horse, a cast of rum, or a bundle of tobacco. But no one would buy him at any price. They wanted nothing to do with such a weak, pitiful, black slave. He was put back in the bottom of the ship with the other sick slaves.

Some time later a British man-of-war captured the slave ship from the Portuguese and freed the slaves. In 1864 at the Canterbury Cathedral, dignitaries from all over England and the world gathered to consecrate a bishop for the Niger. Who was he? Was he some trained scholar from Oxford? No. He was the former black slave who in 1821 no one would even purchase at the marketplace. After the slave ship was rescued by the British, Samuel Adjai Crowther, this black slave, was set free and taken to Sierra Leone where he came under the influence of the preaching about Christ and became a Christian. That former slave later was chosen and consecrated as a bishop. A man, who was despised, rejected and a slave was transformed by the power of Jesus Christ. All are welcomed at the foot of the cross. The writer declares: "He will save us to the uttermost."[23]

CHRIST REIGNS FOREVER

Jesus is also a High Priest who can make intercession for us because he reigns forever. He is at the right hand of God the Father and "ever lives to make intercession for us." The Hebrew author drew on Psalm 110 where he declares that Jesus was not an ordinary priest but one after the order of Melchizedek, who was a mysterious, kingly priest figure before the Levite system of priest was instituted. He had blessed Abraham and had received tithes from Abraham. Melchizedek was a figure surrounded in mystery, whose genealogy was unknown. To the writer of the Book of Hebrews, Jesus Christ is like this ancient king of righteousness. He is the one who is reigning at the right hand of God and is able to make intercession for us.

But that is only a part of the good news of the message of the cross. What happened at the cross of Jesus Christ was not limited to the people who were living then. He continues to give us access into God's presence. He continues to make intercession for us today when we come confessing our sins. He is our eternal priest in heaven who pleads for our forgiveness. You and I can continue to experience the forgiving love and grace of God because of his priestly intercession.

THE ETERNAL LOVE OF GOD

The cross likewise reveals to us the heartbeat of God. What happened at the cross of Jesus was not the only time God had ever been a loving God. God has always been a loving and redemptive God. But for some reason men and women were not able neither to understand nor accept his message of love. The cross of Jesus Christ was a "slice" into time so men and women could see the inner heart of God. God is a loving, suffering God. When you make a chip with an axe into a tree, you are able to see something about the nature of the trees grain of wood. The cross provides an opening into eternity, revealing in time and space, a dimension about God's nature. The Book of Revelation speaks about "the Lamb slain before the foundation of the world." Jesus Christ did not die because God was angry with us and he had to appease God. The Scriptures tell us that God loved the world. Christ died so that you and I might be reconciled to God. Our sin separated us from God, but the death of Jesus reconciled an estranged world.

The other day I saw again a painting which I had not seen for a long time. This painting depicts the cross of Christ lifted high in the heavens above a very calm lake. Beside the lake there is a fishing boat with some men with fishing nets. As I studied that picture of the cross suspended high above the earth, it brought to my mind the message of the eternal dimension of God's sacrificial love. God was in Christ at the cross reconciling the world unto himself. Through the sacrificial death of Christ, the heartbeat of God's eternal love has been disclosed to us.

THE COSTLY DIMENSION OF THE CROSS

The cross also reveals the costly nature of God's sacrifice. We can't assume that our sin doesn't do any harm. Sin put Christ on the cross. Your sins and mine, the deliberate sins of all persons, resulted in his crucifixion. Sin is damaging to our relationship with God, ourselves, and others. We need to be reconciled to God. It was costly to God to come into our world in the unique way that he did. It cost him the humility of the Incarnation. It cost him the rejection of his Son. When he preached a message of love, grace, peace, and that the Kingdom of God was near, he and his message were rejected. It cost him pain, suffering, and death to redeem us. Although it was costly, Jesus, nevertheless, was obedient unto death, even the death on a cross.

John Gossip, the noted Scottish preacher, said that he heard George Adam Smith speak one day in Edinburgh, and, although he could not remember much from his message that day, he did recall one story. Dr. Smith told a story about a fisherman who had put his trawler out from Aberdeen into the stormy sea. While he was out, the waters got so rough that his young son was swept off the small boat into the water. As he looked for his son in the white snarl of boiling water, he saw his son sinking under the high waves, and he knew he was helpless to help his son. "I understood," he said, "for the first time the meaning of a verse I had known from childhood, `Like as a father pities his children, so the Lord pities them that fear Him.'" "And at the Cross," Gossip observes, "we understand what God means when he talks about loving us, begin to take it in that there is nothing that He will not do, no sacrifice He will not make, no suffering that He will shirk, if only He can help us."[24] He was willing to make any sacrifice that we might understand his love.

Why haven't men and women always understood the God about whom the great prophets preached in the Old Testament? I don't know. But they haven't. Why don't people hear the message of Christ today? Why don't they respond to it? Why don't they believe it? Why don't they live by it? I don't know why, but they don't. You don't! I don't! We have heard the message, but if we really responded to it, we, our world, the Church, and our churches would be different. If persons really believed and responded to God's love, would we have the kinds of problems we have today? But we really do not live out a genuine response to such love.

Jesus came into our world to reveal what the nature of God was like. Look at him! LOOK at him. Here is Jesus today. In ancient Israel Jesus reached out to people who were hurting, blind, deaf, or lame, and healed them. His action declared: "God is like this—caring and loving." He reached out to the women of society who had been isolated, categorized and the victims of prejudice and he declared that God is caring. He reached across lines to persons of all races and said that God is loving. He saw people hungry and he fed them and declared that God is concerned. Wherever there was a need, wherever there were hurts, pains, or burdens Jesus reached out to them. Through Jesus' ministry, we get a glimpse of God's love. Sin dug a great chasm that separated us from God. We could not cross that chasm by our own strength or efforts. But Jesus Christ bridged that chasm so we could come into fellowship and communion with God. Sin separates us from God. But Jesus Christ has reconciled us to God so that we can come into his presence.

Frank Stagg in his book on New Testament theology illustrates how the death of Jesus Christ rescues men and women from sin. Suppose a child is lost in a heavy snow and he is unable to get home. Several things could be done. When the father found his child, he could tell his son to follow him. He could give him an example of how to get back home. But one's own example would not be enough. He could leave his son in the snow and go for help. But, of course, if he did that, his son might die. Or, he could take his son's hand and lead him home through the snow. This way the child would be rescued because his father had delivered him. "Christ saves us in his work of deliverance. He does something for us; but more than that, he does something in us."[25]

Jesus Christ reaches out his hand to you and me and brings us into the way of salvation. This is done not just by example, but by laying down life. You and I, by responding to him, have and can receive redemption and grace.

5

EASTER: LIVING BEYOND THE CROSS

The cross closed the door of hope for the early disciples. It was a crushing, staggering blow to them. To see the one whom they had hoped would be the Messiah nailed to a cross in a scandalous way was a deeply shattering experience. On Friday and Saturday the eleven disciples had gathered together in the Upper Room, filled with dejection, defeat, despair and not knowing which way to turn. On Sunday afternoon two of the disciples of Jesus, who were not numbered with the eleven, left Jerusalem with downcast spirits. One of the disciples' name was not even listed, which obviously meant that the person was unknown to the writer of this gospel. One of these disciples is called Cleopas, and some scholars have suggested that the unknown person might have been Cleopas' wife. Maybe they were a couple heading home. We simply don't know for sure. Some have speculated that this unknown disciple might have been Luke himself (Luke 24:13-35). Tradition, however, states that the unknown disciple was a man named Simon. His identity has forever eluded us.

A TRIP TO EMMAUS

Late on the Sunday afternoon following the crucifixion of Jesus these two disciples were walking home toward Emmaus, a city that was located seven miles northwest of Jerusalem. They were walking toward the sunset. The shadows that fell across their pathway that afternoon were shadows of defeat, dejection, and doubt. Their dream that Jesus was the promised Messiah had been crushed to the ground at Calvary. "Let's go back home now and see what we can do" they likely said to each other. "Maybe we can look for another." Matthew had suggested that he might go back to the tax collector's desk. Peter stated that he would return to his work as a fisherman. Two lonely disciples, their minds filled with questions, their spirits crushed, their minds clouded with depression, were returning home to Emmaus to see what they would do now.

Sad and unbelieving, their worst fears had been realized. The death of Jesus seemed so final to them. The words of Job might have echoed in their minds: "If a man dies, will he live again" (Job 14:12-17)? To them there was no "if a man dies." They had witnessed the certainty of death. The death of Jesus had ended their hope of the promised Messiah. His death seemed so final and complete. Then suddenly a stranger appeared and started walking with them. They had not noticed him on the road before, and they did not recognize that this stranger was Jesus.

WHY DID THEY NOT RECOGNIZE JESUS?

That has always been so curious to me. How could that have happened? If these travelers were his disciples, how could they not know that it was Jesus? Did they not recognize his voice? His demeanor? His walk? His words? It has always been staggering for me to try to get a handle on their failure to recognize him. The King James Version read, "Their eyes were holden that they should not know him." For some reason they did not recognize him. Unbelief clouded their perspective. Remember, none of the disciples had been able to understand or accept Jesus' teaching about a crucified Messiah. His death on a cross came as a complete shock to them. Only after the resurrection did they begin to understand his message. He was a stranger.

But don't judge them too quickly. Don't be harsh in your judgment in the fact that they did not recognize Jesus. I wonder how

many times in your life and mine Jesus has come and we have not
recognized him. He came as a stranger and we did not take him in.
He came to us in the outstretched hand of need from some
stranger on a busy city street, in the tears of some friend whose
heart was breaking and we did not have time to listen. He meets
us in the faces of the lonely, ill, hurting, poor, needy, or outcast of
society. I wonder how many times Jesus has come to us and he has
remained a stranger.

Francis of Assisi was petrified of lepers and avoided them out
of fear of contracting leprosy. According to an ancient legend, as
Francis was travelling down the road one day, he met a leper who
was white with the dread disease. The man's body was covered in
sores from his leprosy. At first Francis was terrified and drew back
in horror. But getting himself under control, he walked over to the
leper and embraced him. The leper continued to walk on down the
road. When Francis turned to look back at the leprous man, he was
gone. Francis was convinced that the leper had been the Christ
whom he met that day. I wonder how many times Jesus has come
to us, and he has remained as one unknown, a stranger to us. We,
like these two disciples, did not recognize him.

The stranger listened to these disciples. Have you ever wondered
what they said? They probably shared the dream which they had
had about Jesus. They spoke about a marvelous happening a week
ago when Jesus had come into Jerusalem in great triumph. "He
seemed to be entering the Holy City as the promised Messiah. The
crowds along the road threw palm branches down in his path. They
were shouting: 'Hosanna.' Surely this will be the end of the Roman
occupation of our country. Jesus will be crowned King, and God's
Kingdom will come on earth. The Messiah entered Jerusalem tri-
umphantly. Later Jesus cleansed the temple. What a marvelous act
that was! He pointed out the thieving, hypocritical leaders of worship who had stolen from us for years. He kicked over their money
tables which they had set up in God's house and said that the
temple was a house of prayer, but they had made it a den of rob-
bers. What a great triumphant act!"

"But we were not sure what he meant by his celebration of the Passover with the twelve in that Upper Room. His words sounded strange to us. That night in the darkness of the night soldiers came to the garden with torches flickering. Judas, one of the twelve, was with the temple soldiers and he came over and kissed Jesus. 'I'll never understand that,' Cleopas said. The soldiers grabbed Jesus and led him off for a mock trial before the high priest, the Sanhedrin, Herod and Pilate. Finding him guilty—of what I don't know—they scourged him and then the unspeakable happened. They stretched him out on a cross and crucified him. Soon it was all over and he was dead. We had hoped that this Jesus was the Messiah. But . . . . Then this morning we heard some strange stories. His body was not in the tomb when Peter and John went there. Nobody could find it. Some women said that he had risen, and Mary had seen him. But we can't believe those idle women's tales, can we?"

JESUS SHARES SCRIPTURES WITH THEM

The stranger on the Emmaus Road listened. Then he spoke. His words began as a gentle rebuke. There were no harsh words like, "Don't you remember what I have taught you?" "Why did all of you deny me?" "Where is your faith?" "Stand up and be men." He uttered a gentle rebuke, and then he pointed them to the Scriptures. Have you ever wondered what Scriptures he shared? Did he point them to the Scriptures about the Suffering Servant, or words from Jeremiah, or the Psalms, or passages from Isaiah, and others? He guided them on a pilgrimage through the Scriptures and described how God had worked through the ancient prophets, the notion Israel, and how God had always been a suffering, redemptive God. Did he help them to see that what had happened in the Son being crucified was in keeping with the way God had always expressed his love for his people?

The stranger interpreted the Scriptures to them. But what he gave them was more than just an interpretation; he himself was the Interpreter. He was himself the fulfillment of the law and the prophets. Luther once said: "Christ is the manger of the Scriptures." All Scripture is seen, understood, and interpreted through Christ. He pointed out how God had revealed himself through Christ, and their hearts "burned within them."

These disciples were no strangers to the Scriptures. They had spent their lifetime studying the Scriptures, but like you and me, they had not seen how they pointed them to Christ. Even with all their knowledge of the Scriptures, they did not recognize the Messiah when he came. They had read familiar biblical passages dozens of times but had not seen Christ walking through them. He had been among them and they did not recognize the One for whom they had been looking for centuries. He spoke to them through the Scriptures.

THE NECESSITY OF AN INVITATION

After talking for a long time on the road, they arrived at the disciples' house in Emmaus, and the stranger "appeared to be going further." Isn't that the way Jesus Christ always comes into our lives? He enters our life by knocking on the door of our heart. He will come in, if we will open, but if you and I do not give him an invitation to enter, he will not force his way in. He always reaches the point in our life's journey where he indicates that he wants to go further. If we will not invite him in, he moves on. Jesus is always trying to take us further, into deeper understanding of God, his divine nature, and how we are supposed to serve him. He is always trying to take us further in our knowledge and devotion.

The two disciples constrained him—entreated him—to come and stay the night with them. When they went into the house of the disciples, Jesus sat down at a table with them as their guest. But the guest suddenly became the host. The One who had been invited in as a guest became the host at their table. But that is the way Jesus always acts in the lives of his disciples. When Jesus Christ comes into your life and mine, we can never control, manipulate, or dominate him. He is Lord and Master. He comes into our lives to rule us, guide us, and direct us. The Church he established is never our church. It is always his church. He is always Lord of the church and Lord of our lives. We can't tell him what to do. He instructs us. He is host. He is Lord.

THE BREAKING OF BREAD

Then the stranger took bread, broke it, and gave it to them. Suddenly in that act, in that moment, their eyes were opened. What did they see that opened their eyes? Did they see the nail prints in his hands for the first time as he broke bread? Did their minds recall Jesus' feeding of the five thousand? Did their thoughts race back to the Upper Room where he broke bread, blessed it, and gave to his disciples? Did the breaking of bread remind them of the Lord's Supper? Whatever happened in that moment caused their eyes to be opened and they recognized that the stranger was Jesus. And immediately he disappeared.

C. H. Dodd, one of the great New Testament scholars, spoke to a great throng of people who had gathered in Westminster Abbey on March 15, 1961, on the 350th anniversary of the publication of the authorized version of the Bible, what you and I call the King James Version. At that celebration, the New English Bible was presented as a fresh translation. C. H. Dodd, the General Director of the new translation, spoke about the meticulous work of the host of scholars, but he also reminded the congregation that day that the supreme fact to which the first Christians gave witness was not the cross but the resurrection. The resurrection is the central truth of the Christian faith. Without the resurrection, the cross has no meaning. Our eyes, like those disciples in that ancient village, need to be opened to the reality of the presence of the living Lord.

Susan Coolidge has expressed the truth of Calvary and Easter in these lines:

A song of sunshine through the rain,
    of Spring across the snow:
A balm to heal the hurts of pain,
    A peace surpassing woe.
Lift up your heads, ye sorrowing ones,
    And be ye glad of heart,
For Calvary and Easter Day,
Earth's saddest day and gladdest day,
    Were just three days apart![26]

JESUS GOES BEFORE THEM

Their eyes were opened and they recognized him. When they did, he vanished out of their sight. Now, I have to confess that I don't understand all of the New Testament references to Jesus' vanishing and reappearing, but it is obvious that one of the truths in their message is that it was necessary for the physical Jesus to depart in order for men and women to relate to the risen Lord by faith and not by sight. Our Lord was preparing his disciples for the final withdrawal of his visible presence. Our response to Christ is always by a commitment of faith. We can invite him to abide with us, but we can never contain him, hold him, or keep him. We don't hold him; he holds us. He always goes before us to lead us further.

After Jesus vanished, the story reveals how the disciples' hearts burned within them as they recalled what Jesus had taught them. When they saw the risen Lord, they knew that Jesus was more than a teacher, prophet, revolutionary, or a healer. They got so excited about what they had seen and heard that they ran, I believe, back to Jerusalem to tell others about what they had seen.

THE WONDER OF EASTER

On Easter Sunday, of all Sundays, if you and I can't get excited about the reality of the risen Christ, then we don't really understand what the Christian faith truly is. Ernest Campbell, a former minister at Riverside Church in New York City, told about an experience which happened in a business session several years ago. When the moderator asked if there were any other items of business, a familiar woman stood up. Those present could hear the rustle of feet as the church members recognized this woman. She always stood up at business sessions and asked something that created a stir. "I have got a question," she stated. "What I want to know is what has happened to the trumpets?" "Beg your pardon?" Dr. Campbell responded. "What I want to know is what has happened to the trumpets on Easter Sunday? How come we don't have them any more?"

Easter Sunday ought to be the Sunday that the trumpets blared. Christ is risen! Our lives should vibrate with a sense of excitement and enthusiasm about the fact that he lives! As the emotions of these two disciples were stirred by the risen Christ, we too should be stirred with excitement and joy.

TELLING OTHERS WHAT WE HAVE EXPERIENCED

When these two disciples reached Jerusalem, they shared out of their experience what they had seen and heard. "We have seen the risen Christ," they exclaimed. Isn't genuine religion always that which is shared out of one's personal experience with God? Abraham, having met God, went on a journey into an uncharted world and shared his message of God with others. Moses, having experienced God in a burning bush, went to tell others about his vision. Isaiah, having seen God high and lifted up in the temple, shared his vision with others. Jacob, having wrestled with God by a riverside, went to share his vision with others. Paul, blinded on the Damascus Road by Christ's presence, went later to share that experience with others. All of the disciples of Christ, who had seen the risen Lord, shared with others what they had seen and experienced.

When these two disciples got back to Jerusalem, they found that others there had already seen Christ as well. You and I share in a common experience which others have had with the risen Christ. When was the last time, when at any time, have you shared your experience of Christ with another? If you and I have really experienced the power of Christ, then we have found an inner joy, sensed an inner radiance, have felt a compulsion, and have cultivated a hope—no, a victory over death. If the risen Christ is real to us, we will want to share our experience with others and invite them to participate with us in the joy that we have experienced.

One of my favorite Easter stories is one which Robert Raines tells. When his son was very small, the family had just come home from a Maundy Thursday service at church. His young son, Bobby, crawled up in his father's lap and said: "Daddy, explain to me again what Maundy Thursday is." His father, who was a minister, began to tell his son that Maundy Thursday was the night when Jesus had his last supper with his disciples. "After the supper, Jesus went out to the Garden of Gethsemane, was arrested, and later put to death. Then on Easter Sunday Jesus rose from the grave, and his disciples saw him. He appeared to Mary, Peter, and many others." His young son listened with excitement as his father told the wonder of the Easter story. After his father finished, Bobby looked up at him and asked; "Daddy, will Easter ever happen to me?"[27]

The Christian faith is built on Easter happening to other people. The risen Christ is Lord. You and I can meet him today and be changed by his presence. May our eyes be opened to see the One who comes and continually comes to reveal and bring us the love of God.

6

BEARING YOUR OWN CROSS

Alfred Adler tells a story about two men who met in a railway station in Austria. One of the men was a wino who was begging for money for his next drink. The stranger asked the man who was begging for money for a drink: "How did you get in such a condition? You seem like a man who has many fine gifts." "Ah," he said, "you don't understand. The cards have always been stacked against me in life. My mother died when I was very young. My father beat me up a great deal. In the war I was separated from my family and I never saw them again."

"That's strange," the other man said. "My background was very similar to yours. My mother died when I was very young. My father also was brutal to me, and I was separated from my family in the war. Because of my adverse circumstances I thought I should try to do the best I could to make something of myself." As the two men continued to talk, they discovered that they were brothers! One of them had become an alcoholic and spent his life wandering from one place to another begging for money to get a drink. The other had risen to a significant place in society. Both came out of the same kind of circumstances.

CHOOSING THE COMFORTABLE WAY

We often say, "Gosh, if I just had it easy in life I could do exactly what I wanted. If I just didn't have all of my problems and difficulties, life would be so much better." With that thought in mind, look at the story of Abraham and Lot found in Genesis 13:1-13. They both were wealthy men in their day. In fact, each of them had such large flocks that they could not graze their flocks in the same area. Quarrels began to break out among the herdsmen, and they realized that they needed to separate.

Abraham gave Lot the first choice of land on which to settle. On one side was the Jordan Valley with its fertile green grass and flowing streams. On the other side was the rough mountain terrain, which was not barren like the wilderness nearby, but was not as choice as the Jordan Valley. Lot chose the lush, green valley, which was the easier way. Abraham was left with the mountains which would be a rough and difficult existence. After Lot settled in the valley, notice that the text states that Lot pitched his tent toward Sodom.

It is usually true to life that those who choose the easy, comfortable style of life often pitch their tents toward Sodom, and pleasure soon becomes the chief end in life. In this Old Testament story we find the contrast between two types of life. One way is represented by Lot who chose the comfortable and easy way. The other way of life is the more adventuresome style of living which Abraham chose. Note what is involved in these two choices.

THE SELF-CENTERED APPROACH

Lot's choice was based on a self-centered approach to living. His choice indicated a desire for security. He selected the more fertile land which offered him security and less hardship. Like Lot, most people want absolute security in life. They are really afraid of the future. Our self-centeredness asserts itself. Some have characterized our age as the "me" generation. Many look out only for number one. Their primary question is: "What can I get from life?" Many business executives and church officials state that among the first questions they are asked by college or seminary graduates who are seeking a job is, "What is the retirement plan like?" I am not saying that they shouldn't have a retirement plan or not have any concern about that; but sometimes rather than having any sense of adventure about their job or future vocation they simply want absolute security.

I read a limerick recently which captures this self-absorbed view of life:

> There once was a nymph named Narcissus,
> Who thought himself very delicious;
> So he stared like a fool
> At his face in a pool,
> And his folly today is still with us.[28]

There are a lot of people who go through life with their central thrust being primarily, "What can I get out of life for myself?" The desire for absolute security has caused them to put their basic emphasis on insurance policies, retirement plans, or social security. They think these will guarantee them absolute security. Lewis Carroll, the writer of Through the Looking Glass, has poked holes in our quest for security in a conversation between Alice and the White Knight.

"But you've got a beehive or something like it fastened to the saddle," said Alice.

"Yes, it's a very good beehive," the knight said in a discontented tone, "one of the best kind. But not a single bee has come near it yet. And the other thing is a mouse trap. I suppose the mice keep the bees out, or the bees keep the mice out, I don't know which."

"I was wondering what the mouse trap is for," said Alice.

"It isn't very likely there would be any mice on the horse's back."

"Not very likely, perhaps," said the knight, "but if they do come, I don't choose to have them running all about. You see," he went on after a pause, "it's as well provided for everything."[29]

Ah, some of us naively think that we can provide ourselves with a kind of security that will protect us against every single thing that might possibly happen in life. But life never gives us absolute security, does it?

Lot's choice also represented a more comfortable, easier lifestyle. We don't have to look far to observe that this is basically the choice we want today. We have moved a long way today away from the pioneering, adventuresome spirit that founded our country. Most of us have great difficulty living with any kind of inconvenience. When the electrical power goes off, if it is a hot day or very cold, we have difficulty adjusting to the inconvenience. We are so used to comfort. If the temperature is not exactly right in church—maybe it's too hot or too cold—we are inconvenienced and so complain. Our first goal is comfort.

THE QUEST FOR A COMFORT RELIGION

One of the primary goals which many seek in religion is comfort. What is the most popular kind of religion in our country today? Turn on the tube. You have got it! Most of the television evangelists give us a comfort religion—peace of mind, possibility thinking, or positive thinking. Examine many of their sermon themes: "How Religion Can Remove All Tension from Your Life." "How to Be A Success and Overcome Failure." "How You Can Overcome Stress." "How to Be Free of Worry." "Drop All Anxiety with Faith." Now I am not saying that these are insignificant concerns. But they are a far cry from the gospel! They are far removed from what Jesus Christ described as his way of life. This "pink-pill" approach toward religion has become the style that many have adopted today. Christian Science, for example, has removed the cross completely from their religion. In the sermons or topics about peace of mind, tranquility, ease, and success, do you hear the call to a cross-like way of life? Almost never!

In Aldous Huxley's *Brave New World* the author depicts a futuristic utopian society where the needs of every person were provided for, every decision was made for them, and every comfort and necessity were provided. But the Savage, who is the hero in this novel, finally cries out: "It's too easy. I don't want comfort. I want God. I want poetry. I want real danger. I want freedom. I want goodness."[30] When you have real freedom, there may be dangers, discomforts, and inconvenience. But it is a more authentic way of life.

Several years ago a group of college students were gathering for their picture to be taken for the college annual. The photographer instructed the officers of the Religious Activities Council to gather around the wooden cross which they had. Photographers often want the persons whom they are photographing to be doing something while they take their pictures and he said: "Now be adjusting the cross as I take the picture."

Be adjusting the cross. . . . We have a lot of people who have adjusted the cross. They have adjusted it right out of their lives altogether. They do not want to be disturbed by it, and so they ignore it.

INDIFFERENCE TO OTHERS

In choosing his pathway, Lot also indicated that he was indifferent to what Abraham did. I don't hear any cry from Lot about the hardships that his decision might put on his brother when he had to go to the mountain section. Lot gladly chose the easier way of living, and seemed oblivious to what Abraham had to do. In our society today many live out their lives indifferent to what happens to others. As long as "I" have comfort; as long as "I" have my conveniences; as long as "I" have enough security; and as long as "I" am satisfied, what difference does it make if there are homeless people in our society, families who do not have enough food to put on their table, starving people around the world, or others who are hurting or in need? Indifference is a horrid sin.

C. S. Lewis addresses this sin in his *Screwtape Letters*. He depicts the Devil briefing his nephew, Wormwood, on how to tempt human beings. The goal that you need to establish, he advises him, is not wickedness but indifference. You don't need to persuade people to do evil itself but always keep them busy doing nothing. The important thing is to keep your patient comfortable. Let nothing upset or disturb him. If he becomes the least bit concerned with anything vitally important, keep him thinking about something else that might give him indigestion. "The great thing is to prevent his doing anything . . . . The more often he feels without acting, the less he will be able ever to act, and, in the long run, the less he will be able to feel."[31]

If we live our lives in an uncaring way, then we will never seek to meet the needs of anyone else. Do you remember when Flip Wilson was a regular on television? One of the characters he impersonated was a deacon. The deacon was talking to a man one day and asked him what his religion was. "I am a Jehovah By-Stander," he replies: "A Jehovah By-Stander?" "Yes, they wanted me to be a Witness, but I didn't want to get involved!" Why, he is characteristic of so many of us, isn't he? We want to be Christian by-standers or by-sitters. We don't want to get involved. Getting involved in human need takes time. We might get hurt. It might even cost us some money, effort, or energy!

THE ADVENTURESOME WAY OF FAITH

Abraham chose the more adventuresome way—the way of faith. He chose the way where he was willing to take risks, to be a pioneer. He had gone out searching for God's city, which was without foundation. He began by taking a journey of faith. Now rather than taking the easy path into the fertile valley, he climbed again to the mountain peaks and labored strenuously for God. I don't think God always calls us to the most comfortable places. I don't understand God's ways. Who among us doesn't want ease and comfort?

Sometimes God, however, calls us to difficult places with hardships and burdens. These may be places where no one else wants to go. As true Christians we must, MUST remain open to that sense of call and not attempt to program how God will direct us. Jesus calls us to a way that is radically different from the world. He calls us to move from the easy plane of absolute comfort and security to a higher way—the way of sacrificial service, the way of love, concern, and ministry. The cross is not just an inconvenience in our faith. The cross is a way of life.

Jesus said, "If any person will come after me, let him or her get their priorities right." You do that by denying self. "Oh, now wait a minute," we want to cry. That cuts against everything we are being taught today. We are in a society where we want to say, "I'm o.k. You're o.k." "I'm alright." What Jesus is telling us, though, is that life is never to be focused merely on what I can get out of it in a selfish way. Our priority needs to be instead, "How I can utilize my gifts in God's service." The paradoxical truth is that we find our real self only in giving that self to God. You will never find your real self—the potential self within you—as long as you focus on self-centeredness. When you and I give our inner selves for God to be used for a higher cause and ministry, then we will find ourselves.

THE SACRIFICIAL WAY

When you get your priorities right, then you will find a pattern for life. Jesus states that our pattern for life is "to take up our cross." In the day of Jesus, people knew what that statement meant. They often saw men being led to be crucified outside the city. Varus, a Roman general, stopped a revolt in Galilee and crucified two thousand men and lined the roadsides of Galilee with their crosses. Each one of these men had to bear the crossbeam to which he was going to be nailed to the spot of crucifixion. When Jesus said, "Take up your cross," his listeners had witnessed this event often. Jesus has called us to a different way of living—the cross-like way. It is a call to live sacrificially in ministry for him.

Isn't this what Dietrich Bonhoeffer was trying to tell us when he wrote about the church offering cheap grace? "Cheap grace is the preaching of forgiveness without requiring repentance, baptism without church discipline, communion without confession, absolution without personal confession," he declares. "Cheap grace is grace without discipleship, grace without the cross, grace without Jesus Christ living and incarnate."[32] To be a disciple of Jesus Christ is demanding. It is a curse on the church to take the cross out of its preaching and ministry.

If you are willing to "take up your cross," then Jesus calls you to discipleship with his words, "Follow me." Jesus issues us a call to obedience. You are not called to see what you can get out of life or how happy you can be, but to follow the way of Jesus. Jesus himself was soon going to lay down his life. He was calling his disciples to "come follow me" and be willing to do the same. Is that what Bonhoeffer meant in his famous statement? "When Christ calls a man, He bids him come and die."[33] Many of the early Christian disciples did die for Christ. He is calling us to die first to self-centeredness and let the power of his risen presence carry us into greater ministry.

"Costly grace," Bonhoeffer notes, "is *costly* because it calls us to follow, and it is grace because it calls us to follow *Jesus Christ*." He continues:

> It is costly because it cost a man his life, and it is grace because it gives a man the only true life. It is costly because it condemns sin, and grace because it justifies the sinner. Above all, it is *costly* because it cost God the life of his Son: "Ye were bought at a price," and what has cost God much cannot be cheap for us. Above all, it is *grace* because God did not reckon his Son too dear a price to pay for our life.[34]

The call to follow Jesus is a demand for daily self-denial. How can you die daily for Christ? Jesus' call is to a sacrificial way of living. It is a summons to a continuous denial of self-centeredness. The call to follow him is not just a one-time call to commitment. You do not make a single commitment to Christ in a moment and it is all over. "I'm a Christian! Isn't that wonderful!" you say. Christ's summons to discipleship is a call to begin living the Christlike way of life every day. Take up your cross daily.

Joseph Hocking, in a novel entitled *The Trampled Cross*, told about a British soldier who was captured by Arabs during some desert fighting. The Arabian chieftain took two sticks and placed them in the shape of a cross, tied them together and laid them in the sand. Then he turned to the Christian and said; "There is the symbol of your faith. Trample on it, and we shall let you go free."

SHUNNING THE CALL TO DISCIPLESHIP

Before you dismiss that as something that can never happen to you, think about how often you and I put aside our call to discipleship. Jesus Christ has called us to a way of life which demands sacrificial living, and this call is still an offense to us today. Oh, we don't mind hearing sermons about the cross, as long as they tell us about what God did for us in Christ. We don't mind hearing songs about the cross. We don't even mind singing songs about the cross or depicting the cross in paintings, sculptures, stained glass windows, or wearing the image around our nicks or on our lapels. But when we begin to realize that the cross is supposed to be a way of life, it is even more offensive to us today. Few people really live a sacrificial kind of life. But Jesus has called us to the cross-like way of life.

CHOOSING THE CROSS-LIKE WAY

In the last century, Albert Schweitzer has exemplified sacrificial dedication. Although he was acclaimed as a noted philosopher, theologian, organist, musicologist, minister, and professor, he believed something was missing from his life. The void in his life was filled when he prepared himself to go as a medical missionary to Lambarene, Africa. Schweitzer believed that he needed to make some acknowledgement to God for the blessings he had received. In his autobiography, he states that he was stabbed awake one morning with the realization that "I must not accept this happiness as a matter of course, but must give something in return for it . . . I tried to settle what meaning lay hidden for me in the saying of Jesus: `Whosoever would save his life shall lose it, and whosoever shall lose his life for my sake and the Gospels shall save it'. . . . In addition to the outward, I now had inward happiness."[35] When our lives are directed inwardly, our concerns are selfish, and we cannot see beyond our own immediate needs or desires. So, we rush from one arena of life to another seeking satisfaction and fulfillment.

"The Schweitzers in our world are rare," someone says. Yes, but Albert Schweitzer does not stand alone. Others, from the age of the apostle Paul to our present era, have marched that sacrificial way. Remember Francis of Assisi, the man of peace and poverty; Florence Nightingale, the founder of the modern nursing movement; William Booth, whose Salvation Army circles the world; Martin Luther, the church reformer; Toyohiko Kagawa, the Japanese social reformer; Tom Dooley, the medical doctor to Southeast Asia; Ann Sullivan Macy, who lifted Helen Keller out of a pit of personal darkness; Mother Teresa, who labored in India; Martin Luther King, Jr., who dreamed of a new, free society for all people. The list could go on. They lost themselves in worthy causes beyond themselves. They found the higher way and dared to walk in it.

I have seen others who have walked the paradoxical way of Jesus. They have received little recognition, if any, for their service—no national or world applause. They saw a need and moved in to help, in a quiet, unheralded manner. You know their faces in your community. In my community, I can see a retired school principal, in her eighties, walking to church in the snow to teach a middle-aged black man how to read, as she has taught hundreds before him. I see a man, whose work schedule is demanding, yet who gives many hours each week to the Boys' Club. I see a couple who bring international students into their home and give them a place where they are loved. I see another couple, going week after week to nursing homes and talking, listening, and playing with the patients.

Many others could join this list. They have committed their lives in a quiet manner to the Christlike way. These are the kind of people who have found the direction of God in ordinary living. These are people who "have bloomed where they were planted" and have not spent this time fantasizing about what they could do "if — ." They have concluded that the problems of life demand daily attention and are not overcome usually in spectacular ways but by plain hard work. They are aware that they cannot solve all the problems of the world or even in their own community, but they have committed themselves to attacking a problem, a part of a problem, if you like, where they live. They are aware that they may not lift the whole burden of sin and suffering from the back of humanity, but they will get under the load so that others will feel some benefit from their efforts.

"The paradoxical thing is," Jesus said, "that you find your life by losing it." You find life by losing it in service. You save your life by giving it up. You will save your life by spending it in service. As you die to selfishness, you find rebirth. In ministering to others, you find what real life really is.

When I was a teenager I discovered the lines of a poem which have echoed in my mind through the years. They express our call to sacrificial living.

> I had walked life's way with an easy tread,
> Had followed where comforts and pleasures led,
> > Until one day in a quiet place
> > I met the Master face to face.

> With station, and rank, and wealth for my soul,
> Much thought for my body, but none for my soul,
> > I had entered to win in life's big race,
> > When I met the Master face to face.

> I had built my castles and reared them high,
> With their towers had pierced the blue of the sky.
> > I had sworn to rule with an iron mace,
> > When I met the Master face to face.

I met Him and knew Him and blushed to see
That His eyes full of sorrow were fixed on me.
I faltered and fell at his feet that day,
While my castles melted and vanished away.

Melted and vanished and in their place
Naught else did I see but the Master's face.
And I cried aloud, 'Oh, make me meet
To follow the steps of Thy wounded feet,'
My thought is now for the souls of men.
I have lost my life to find it again.
Ere since one day in a quiet place
I met the master face to face.[36]

If you have met the Master face to face, he has called you and
he has called me to walk in the Christlike way. We are to take up
our cross and follow him. It is a call to discipleship. Let us hear
that call and follow.

7

The Church Under the Cross

Recently I was talking with a minister friend of mine as we were both preparing for the Lenten/Easter season. He observed how difficult it was for him to think about preaching on the cross. I understand something of his reluctance and timidity in speaking about such a theme. But I have been daring enough in my ministry to try and focus attention upon the cross of Jesus. It may not be easy. But, as a minister, I *must*. There is no way I can possibly write about all that is involved in the great message of the cross in a few pages. Thousands of books have been written about the cross; thousands of sermons have been preached on it. Yet all of them have only touched the edge of the truth contained in its message.

The gospel writers struggled to understand why Jesus was crucified, and the Apostle Paul, without hesitation, put the cross at the center of his preaching. If the church is to be the authentic Church—*authentic* Church—the cross will always be at the center of our preaching and way of life. The church cannot really exist as "the Church" without the memory and the impact of the cross being a vital part of our message and ministry.

The Church Is Called to Remember

We all know how important memory is to us. In our national life we have had various slogans through the years which call us to remember certain events of our past. On February 15, 1898 the ship *Maine* was sunk in the Havana Harbor, and a rallying cry went around our country, "Remember the Maine." When some of our countrymen were killed at the Alamo, the cry to rally our country against the Spanish was, "Remember the Alamo." When the Japanese bombed Pearl Harbor, the cry went up: "Remember Pearl Harbor." Now today whenever our country begins to think about sending troops to battle in a distant land, the cry arises: "Remember Viet Nam" and "remember Iraq and Afghanistan."

We all know the importance of remembering. We know how significant remembering is at the time of a birthday, anniversary, Christmas or some other special occasion. The Jewish people were constantly reminded to remember. They were told to remember what God had done for them at the Exodus. "Remember," they were told, "how God has set you free from slavery, brought you into a new land, and made you a new people." The Christian church focuses at the Lord's Table on bread and wine and is called to remember what our Lord has done for us through his death. Through the years to come, Christians are called to remember that the cross is at the center of our faith.

I acknowledge that the message of the cross is still a difficult word for many people to accept today. As the cross was originally an offense and a stumbling block to the ancient Jews and Greeks, many of us find today that it continues to be an offense or trap that keeps us from understanding or living the Christlike way.

THE CONTINUING PERSUASION OF SIN

Why? Well, one reason, I believe, is the awful power and persuasion of sin. Some fathers have grown gray overnight, and mothers have had their hearts broken by the actions of their children. Parents who have teenagers soon realize the power of peer groups, and how quickly a child can be influenced by another and give his or her life to the way of drugs, alcohol, or casual sex. Soon they are trapped by their hold.

Many seem to wink at the awesome power of sin. They seem to have no sense of right or wrong. Almost no one can instruct them to live otherwise. "If I enjoy doing it, it's o.k." "I want to have fun." "Whatever makes me feel good, I will do it." They can't seem to understand the deceit of sin. Like Br'er Rabbit and the Tar Baby we continue to stick ourselves to the power of sin until we are so absorbed by it that we cannot get free from its hold. Who among us does not have some dark corner of his or her mind where lurks the awful reality of unconfessed sins, or sins of prejudice, bigotry, jealousy, envy, or many others. Sometimes we avoid the cross simply because we don't want to deal with our sinfulness.

REMOVING THE CROSS

But on another level we need to observe that many nominal Christians have removed the cross from the church. As E. Stanley Jones once said, "Many have been inoculated with a mild form of Christianity and they are immune to the real thing." Unfortunately, that is true. For many nominal Christians their basic approach to religion is to ask: "What can *I* get out of religion?" The church is perceived as a great community club where I can pick and choose whatever I want from its selection. It is there to be used at my convenience. "The church exists for *me*. I make no commitment to it." "I don't give any time, effort, energy, or money to it. It is there for *my* consumption, to meet *my* needs."

I received a folder in the mail several years ago from a new church which was being started in the east end of Louisville, Kentucky. Among other things in the brochure about the new church were these words: "A simple promise. Promises are easy to make but hard to keep. That is why the new church family of ——makes only one simple promise—'A positive and enjoyable Experience.' That's it! No strings attached. Come and go without any obligations—just enjoy yourselves."

That's church? That represents the heresy of our day! Too many want a church with no strings attached! And many today have bought into this philosophy about church. It is a sad commentary on the church today.

Martin Marty, in an article in the *Christian Century* pointed out how many books and articles have been written recently to persuade the mainline churches of America to emulate the Pentecostal evangelistic approach which these televangelists have been giving us today. Celebrities, he noted, have been created by this kind of "exciting" media, and its masters have mastered the media. They knew how to use computers and the television media, while the mainline Christians did not know how to plug in the audiovisual device in Sunday School classrooms. Not to have this knowledge was considered or implied as being immoral, unfaithful, or unevangelical.

Then Marty went on to observe:

> And now we are coming to a period when, after Roberts and Robertson; Jim and Jimmy, and the lesser-known adulterous whistle-blowers, shadows and stigmas have encircled T.V. ministries. It is now time to ask whether these ministries failed precisely because they offered something other than the gospel, in the name of the gospel; something other than the cross, in the name of the cross; something such as cheap grace to go with easy success?[37]

THE CHURCH'S CALL TO COMMITMENT

This kind of shallow, superficial approach to Christianity will always result in nominal Christians. Whenever or wherever we offer religion with no strings attached, no cost, and no commitment, we are giving cheap grace! As long as the church lifts up a hollow, aluminum foil cross instead of a heavy wooden cross, we will always be guilty of heresy in the message we present to the world. Jesus said, "Foxes have holes, and the birds of the air have nests, but the Son of man has nowhere to lay his head" (Luke 9:58). "Straight is the gate, and narrow is the way which leads to life" (Matt.7:14). "If anyone would come after me, let him deny himself and take up his cross and follow me" (Matt. 16:24). Jesus did not always have ease, comfort and peace of mind. There were times when he wrestled al night long and was unable to sleep.

I heard a young minister say one day, as he pointed to his new car. "God has given me this Cadillac." The thought flashed in my mind, "That's amazing. God has given you a Cadillac, and he gave his own son a cross." The attitude of equating financial and material blessings with the blessings of following the Christlike way is without foundation in the teaching of Jesus. Anyone who desires to follow Christ needs to be aware of the cost involved in following Jesus Christ.

CHRIST'S CALL TO DISCIPLESHIP

Jesus was never interested merely in trying to draw crowds of people around him. One of the heresies of our day is to assume that if you have large crowds you have a great church. Jesus warned the crowds around him to be aware of "the sandpaper edge" in following him in discipleship. To the crowds he exclaimed: "You must be willing to forsake father and mother, brother and sister to follow me" (Luke 14:26). To Nicodemus, the great religious leader, Jesus might have said: "I am flattered that you want to talk to me." But, no, he declared to Nicodemus: "You must be born again." To the rich young ruler, who came to him seeking advise on finding eternal life, Jesus didn't say: "Welcome to my band. It is so good to have you. We can use your money. We need you." Instead he said, "Go and sell all you have and give to the poor and come, follow me."

Jesus was interested in making disciples and not attracting crowds of people. He was interested in disciples who were willing to take up a cross and live his way of life. The medicine of the church always has a warning on its label which reads, "Repent and be converted." If you and I would follow Jesus Christ, we must be transformed. Our lives are to be made over in his image and we are to become different persons as we follow in his way. To be a disciple of Jesus means that we can't have everything in our lives just like we might want it. We cannot cling to our prejudices, bigotry, or selfishness. Jesus always makes demands and often causes inconveniences. We now seek to see life from his perspective. Paul warns the Corinthians and us in II Corinthians 5:17-21 about "accepting the grace of God in vain." In vain? Yes, as George Beasley-Murray wrote, "Paul was deeply concerned that his converts should not abandon the true gospel for a counterfeit version of it."[38]

In the Passion Play at Oberammergau, Anton Lang played the part of Jesus for years. One night, following a performance of the play, some tourists came back to the dressing room of Lang and tried to lift the cross he carried in the play but found it too heavy. "Why," they asked, "do you make the cross so heavy?" "I could not play my part," he replied, "unless I felt the weight of the cross." For the church to be the Church, it must be reminded that the cross bears heavily on our back in genuine discipleship.

THE RECONCILIATION OF THE CROSS

Paul declares in II Corinthians 5 that reconciliation by the cross of Christ is at the center of the Church's message. Reconciliation begins in our awareness of the reality and power of sin in our lives. For some of us, sin is simply a matter of indifference. We are caught in the stream of life and float along seemingly unaware that we are sinners. We drift toward destruction like we were in a boat, enjoying life, unaware of the danger that lurks before us in the approaching waterfall. For most of us, our sin is basically self-centeredness. Like a spider, we spin our webs out of ourselves. We see life in terms of what is good primarily for "me" and "my" surroundings. As someone has observed, "We are our own worst enemies."

Charlie Brown was reading the paper to Lucy one day and he observed: "It says here that young people of today don't believe in any causes. . ." "That's not true at all!" Lucy asserts. "I believe in a cause. . . I believe in ME! I'm my own cause! If I'm not a cause, what is? I believe in the cause of good ol' me! THAT'S the cause I believe in! I'M THE BEST CAUSE I KNOW. AND I BELIEVE IN THAT CAUSE! I'M THE. . ." Charlie Brown walks off saying, "Good grief!"[39]

And good grief it should be! Because that is as far as some people ever get—only concern for self. Others are burdened down with the load of guilt that weights upon them like a heavy chain that shackles them and crushes them to the ground with its load. Guilt hangs heavily on their heart and they seek to find relief from that burden.

Reconciliation is one of Paul's words to expound the message of God's love and grace. Reconciliation in Paul's mind is a word that encompasses all that is involved in redemption, forgiveness, the costly nature of grace, and the restoration of personal friendship with God. Paul's phrase, "In Christ God was reconciling the world to himself" (II Cor. 5:19), encompasses the saving work of Christ. Reconciliation is Paul's message to us about the supreme revelation of the eternal love of God which we have seen at the cross. We also see at the cross the obedience and humility of Jesus, who was willing to lay down his life that we might understand and experience the love of God. At the cross we see the vicarious gift of life, the One who gave life on behalf of another. We see the extent of sacrifice at the cross in the One who became a "sin offering" for us. He was also representative man, the new Adam. The One who died at the cross continues to make intercession for us at the right hand of his Father. In faith we respond to what God has done for us at the cross of Christ.

RESPONDING TO THE CROSS

Sometimes I think that all of our explanations are inferior and inadequate in expressing what Christ has done for us at the cross. Our best response is simply to kneel before that cross and bow before the mystery of what God has done for our redemption in

Christ. We follow the light we have and with our limited understanding of such love, knowing that we can never explain fully or
finally what God has done at the cross. But we can never forget
the extent of such costly love. The Son of Man, the Suffering Servant, the Second Adam, our sin offering, and the Lamb slain from
the foundation of the world all testify to the reconciling work of
Christ.

Paul continues in II Corinthians 5 by reminding us that as
Christians we are also called to a ministry of reconciliation. Paul's
rallying cry was "in Christ." More than fifty-four times in his
epistles Paul used the phrase "in Christ." It is almost his definition
of a Christian. If one is in Christ, he or she is remade; one is radically new. Christ has gone to the roots of that person's existence
and made that individual over again. If one is in Christ, he or she
is out of himself or herself. As Paul walked down the Damascus
Road, he met the Christ and his life was forever different. When a
person is "in Christ," a new creation has occurred.

Paul makes a reference that he knew Christ "according to the
flesh" at one time. Scholars are not certain what Paul meant by this
statement. It is likely a reference to Paul's view of Jesus before he
was converted. Did he mean that he knew Christ whom some were
projecting as an earthly Messiah? Did he understand Christ to be
a heretic as many of the religious leaders believed him to be then?
Had he seen or heard Jesus teach in Jerusalem? Had he actually
seen the physical Jesus?

Paul's use of this phrase is unclear, but we do know that he had
experienced a new understanding of Christ on the Damascus Road.
And that experience changed his life forever. He now saw
everything from a new vantage point. He had become a new creation. The old things had passed away and he now lived a completely new way of life. He had received a new motive. His old
motive was to see what he could do for himself. His new motive
was to live life in the name of Christ. His old way was self-centered;
his new way was Christ-centered.

He had a new perspective—the love of Christ constrained him.
Christ the pleader and God the beseecher entreated him to walk a

new path. Having responded to the imploring love of God, he in turn beseeches others to come to Christ. He was an ambassador for Christ, one who was sent to carry the message of the love for Christ to others. He was sent to share the good news of what God had done in Jesus Christ with others.

A MINISTRY OF SERVICE

What form does this ministry for Christ take? The church under the cross will have a ministry that takes the form of a servant. Just as Jesus was obedient unto death, even the death of the cross, so he has called his disciples to a servant ministry. Jesus took a towel and a basin and washed the feet of his disciples. He said, "I have given you an example that you should do unto others as I have done to you." Jesus reminded his disciples, "If anyone would be first, he must be last of all and servant of all" (Mark 10:43-44). He has called us to a ministry not to see what we can get out of it for ourselves but what we can do in service for him. A servant of Christ will not be power hungry or status conscious. As a servant, he or she decreases that the Master might increase.

To serve in the name of Christ means that sometimes life gets difficult. Ministry is not always easy. Did you know that when William Carey, after many years of trying to become a missionary, finally arrived in India he labored for seven years before there was a Hindu convert? I read about some missionaries in the Yukon who worked for fifteen years before they had a single convert. Now ask, "Were they successful?" By whose standards? We have taken the Madison Avenue notion of success and baptized it as the standard to judge what it means to be successful as a church. Remember, Jesus did not call us to be successful but to be faithful. Too many have drawn the world's criteria for success and tried to use it to measure the success of the church.

But we have not been called to be like the world but to be like Christ. Christ has called us to follow him as servants. An inner-city mission like Jefferson Street Baptist Chapel in Louisville, Kentucky, may never have a convert. But are they not ministering effectively in the name of Christ as they reach out to the homeless, lonely, ill and destitute of our society? Numbers cannot be the true measure of authentic ministry.

Jesus has not called us to be successful but to be faithful. Could we say that our Lord by the world's standards was successful? What about Peter, James, John, or Paul? They all ended up dying as martyrs for the cause of Christ. But if the cross is not accepted, then the church is not faithful to its calling.

THERE ARE RISKS IN FOLLOWING CHRIST

Sometimes his way will be hard and difficult, but Christ challenges us to take risks in his name. If we are really seeking to follow Christ and serve in his name, then we will realize that his servant way involves risks. If we are going to serve Christ, we will have to be willing to risk being misunderstood, or even rejected. We will walk near the edge of heresy to gain new truth and new insight. No ship was designed to remain anchored in the harbor. It was built to be launched out on the sea and set sail. When we hug the shore of security, we never effectively serve Christ.

One night a liner was wrecked on a reef off the coast of New England. As the Coast Guard went out to rescue those in the water, one of the young men looked at the fierceness of the ocean and cried to the captain. "Sir, the wind is offshore and the tide is running out. Of course we can go out, but what good will it do? Against the wind and the tide we cannot come back." All the captain said was, "Launch the boat. We have to go out. We don't have to come back."

When the church is really the Church of Jesus Christ, it will be willing to risk venturing into the world. It will be willing to suffer inconvenience, endure hostility, or step into a dark, untried way. It will risk speaking to a person whom others might not care about, or helping someone who might prove difficult or unappreciated. The Servant Church will risk laughter, ridicule, mockery or criticism. It will speak out for Christ even when it is not popular. It will go out of its way to help another. The Church under the cross will risk breaking new pathways, attempt new ministries, be open to new discoveries from God, and be willing to go wherever God leads without restrictions. A Servant Church will express compassion, care, understanding, sympathy, and love. It will follow its Lord, who by his words, life, and death, modeled the way of the Suffering Servant.

Whenever the church really understands the ministry of Christ, it will accept cost and risk. The church of Jesus Christ does not say to our Lord's disciples, "Come, sit. It doesn't make any difference what you do." He calls us to take up our cross and be ambassadors of reconciliation in our actions and words. Vincent Taylor in his book, *The Cross of Christ*, has expressed that truth this way. "Perhaps our greatest need today, if we would rise above the poverty of much of our worship, is to experience once more the wonder of reliance upon Christ's ceaseless saving ministry, which is the true centre of Christian devotion and the abiding source of Christian living."[40] The cross needs to be at the center of our life. If our Lord gave his life, are we not challenged to give our lives in devotion and ministry for him.

Eric Rust told about visiting Laacher, which was the burial place of many kings. In the royal chapel there was a strange fitting in the reading desk of the pulpit. Hidden inside the cross on the pulpit was a microphone. What a parable about life.[41] The cross, when really understood, becomes a microphone through which the voice of Christ and the voices of his disciples spread the good news of God's grace everywhere.

The cross of Jesus Christ declares that God has reconciled human-kind to himself. The cross reveals to us the costly nature of sin, the love of God, the sacrifice, self-denial, and surrender of Christ, and the limitless grace of the Father. Having been reconciled to God by Christ, we are challenged to share this message of love with others and to live the Christlike, cross-like way of life. It is not the easy life, but I am convinced, it is the Christian way. We bow before the mystery of the cross and follow in its light.

ENDNOTES

1. F. W. Dillistone, *The Christian Understanding of Atonement* (London: James Nisbet and Co., 1968), 1-2.
2. William Law, *A Serious Call to a Devout and Holy Life* (London: J. M. Dent & Sons, 1955), 223.
3, H. Wheller Robinson, *Redemption and Revelation* (London: Nisbet & Co., 1942), 280.
4. Jürgen Moltmann, *The Crucified God* (New York: Harper & Row, 1974), 1.
5. Quoted in Harold Cooke Phillips, *Preaching with Purpose and Power*, edited by Don M. Aycock (Macon, GA: Mercer University Press, 1982), 279.
6. Emil Brunner, *The Mediator* (Philadelphia: The Westminster Press, 1957), 504.
7. Carl Braaten, *Stewards of the Mysteries* (Minneapolis: Augsburg Publishing House, 1983), 43.
8. Isaac Watts, "When I Survey the Wondrous Cross," *Hymns for the Living Church*, edited by Donald P, Hustad (Carol Stream, Illinois: Hope Publishing Co., 1982), 148-149.
9. Lenore Johnson, *Jesus Is* (New York: Harper and Row, 1971), 3.
10. Frank Stagg, "Philippians" *The Broadman Bible Commentary*, vol. 11 (Nashville: Broadman Press, 1971), 196.
11. D. M. Baillie, *God Was in Christ* (New York: Charles Scribner's Sons, 1948), 126.
12. Fred Craddock, *Philippians* (Atlanta: John Knox Press, 1985), 37.
13. Frederick Buechner, *The Hungering Dark* (New York: The Seabury Press, 1969), 11-13.
14. Shusaku Undo, *Silence,* translated by William Johnson (Tokyo: The Charles E. Tuttle Co., 1969), 95-96.
15. W. D. Edwards, W. J. Gabel and F. E. Hosmer, "On the Physical Death of Jesus Christ," *The Journal of the American Medical Association* (March 21, 1986), 1455-1463.
16. Elizabeth Barrett Browning, "Cowper's Grave," *Poems*, Volume II, (New York: James Miller, 1862), 225.

17. Carlyle Marney, *He Became Like Us* (New York: Abingdon Press, 1964), 46-47.
18. Nicholas Wolterstorff, *Lament for a Son* (Grand Rapids: William B. Eerdmans, 1987), 67-68.
19. Martin E. Marty, *A Cry of Absence* (San Francisco: Harper & Row, 1983), 39-40.
20. J. Wallace Hamilton, *Who Goes There?* (Westwood, New Jersey: Fleming H. Revell Co., 1958), 115.
21. L. D. Johnson, *The Morning After Death* (Nashville: Broadman Press, 1978), 113.
22. Wolterstorff, *Lament for a Son*, 76.
23. James Hastings, editor, *The Great Text of the Bible*, vol. XVIII (Grand Rapids: Wm. B. Eerdmans Co., n.d.), 357.
24. Arthur John Gossip, *The Galilean Accent* (Edinburgh: T. T. & Clark, 1926), 142.
25. Frank Stagg, *New Testament Theology* (Nashville: Broadman Press, 1962), 147-148.
26. Charles L. Wallis, editor. *Lenten-Easter Sourcebook* (New York: Abingdon Press, 1961), 160.
27. Robert A. Raines, *Success Is a Moving Target* (Waco: Word Books, Publisher, 1975), 119.
28. John Piper, "Is Self-Love Biblical?" *Christianity Today*, 1977.
29. Lewis Carroll, *Alice's Adventures in Wonderland and Through the Looking Glass* (New York: Barnes & Nobles Classics, 2004), 240.
30. Aldous Huxley, *Brave New World* (New York: Bantam, 1945), 163.
31. C. S. Lewis, *The Screwtape Letters* (London: Fontana Books, 1956), 69-70.
32. Dietrich Bonhoeffer, *The Cost of Discipleship* (London: SCM Press, 1959), 36.
33. *Ibid.*, 79.
34. *Ibid.*, 37.
35. Albert Schweitzer, *Out of My Life and Thought* (New York: Holt, Reinhart, and Winston, 1961), 85.
36. James Gilchrist Lawson, compiler, *The Best-Loved Religious Poems* (New York: Fleming H. Revell Co., 1933), 174-175.
37. Martin E. Marty, "Some Lessons Not to Take," *The Christian Century* (March 16, 1988), 295.
38. G. R. Beasley-Murray, "2 Corinthians" in *The Broadman Bible Commentary*, vol. II (Nashville: Broadman Press, 1971), 46.
39. Robert L. Short, *The Gospel According to Peanuts* (Richmond, VA: John Knox Press, 1965), 60.

40. Vincent Taylor, *The Cross of Christ* (London: Macmillan & Co. 1956), 104.
41. Eric C. Rust, *The Word and the Words* (Macon, Georgia: Mercer University Press, 1982), 127.

Also from Energion Publications

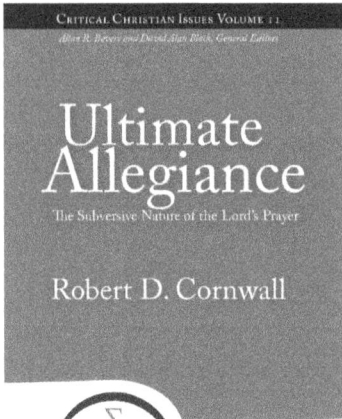

The most recited prayer is performed more often than it is prayed. Bob Cornwall thoughtfully challenges us to recognize the subversive nature of the words we speak. When we truly pray the Lord's Prayer, God pushes us to worship deeply, live bravely, trust fully, forgive freely, and celebrate joyfully. This book is for those who are willing to honestly question their ultimate allegiance.

Brett Younger
Associate Professor of Preaching
McAfee School of Theology,
Atlanta

"To read and interpret the Bible for oneself is a Protestant prerogative, but to read it well requires reliable guides. Bruce Epperly is an able co-conspirator of the Spirit and the church, leading us through Philippians to find the joy of the high calling of Christ Jesus."

Rev. Dr. George A. Mason
Senior Pastor
Wilshire Baptist Church
Dallas, Texas

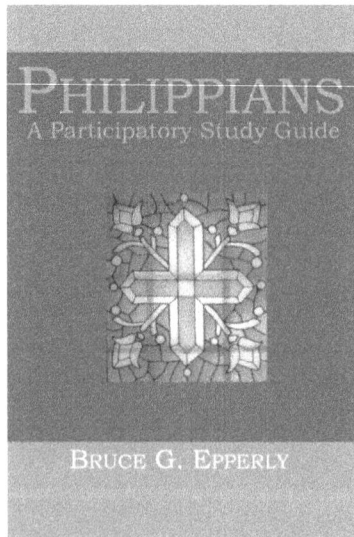

More from Energion Publications

Personal Study

The Jesus Paradigm	$17.99
Finding My Way in Christianity	$16.99
When People Speak for God	$17.99
Holy Smoke, Unholy Fire	$14.99
Not Ashamed of the Gospel	$12.99
Evidence for the Bible	$16.99
Christianity and Secularism	$16.99
What's In A Version?	$12.99
Christian Archy	$9.99
Ultimate Allegiance	$9.99

Christian Living

Daily Devotions of Ordinary People – Extraordinary God	$19.99
Directed Paths	$7.99
Grief: Finding the Candle of Light	$8.99
I Want to Pray	$7.99
Soup Kitchen for the Soul	$12.99

Bible Study

"In the Original Text It Says"	$9.99
Learning and Living Scripture	$12.99
To the Hebrews: A Participatory Study Guide	$9.99
Revelation: A Participatory Study Guide	$9.99
The Gospel According to St. Luke: A Participatory Study Guide	$8.99
Ephesians: A Participatory Study Guide	$9.99
Philippians: A Participatory Study Guide	$9.99
Identifying Your Gifts and Service: Small Group Edition	$12.99
The Character of Our Discontent	$12.99
Why Four Gospels?	$11.99

Theology

God's Desire for the Nations	$18.99
Out of This World: An Assessment of Christian Community	$24.99
From Inspiration to Understanding	$24.99

Generous Quantity Discounts Available

Energion Publications — P.O. Box 841

Gonzalez, FL 32560

Website: http://energionpubs.com

Phone: (850) 525-3916

www.ingramcontent.com/pod-product-compliance
Lightning Source LLC
Chambersburg PA
CBHW051735040426
42447CB00008B/1142